Nelson Handwriting

NELSON HANDWRITING

Primary Teachers' Manual

ALEXANDER INGLIS B.Sc., Dip. Ed., F.E.I.S.
and E. H. GIBSON B.Sc.

Consultant

Dr DOUGLAS M. McINTOSH M.A., B.Sc., Ph. D., F.E.I.S., F.R.S.E., O.B.E.

NELSON

THOMAS NELSON AND SONS LTD

Lincoln Way Windmill Road Sunbury-on-Thames Middlesex TW16 7HP
P.O. Box 73146 Nairobi Kenya
P.O. Box 943 95 Church Street Kingston 5 Jamaica
308-312 Lockhart Road, Golden Coronation Building 2nd Floor
Blk A Hong Kong
29 Jalan Bangau Singapore 28

THOMAS NELSON (AUSTRALIA) LTD
19-39 Jeffcott Street West Melbourne Victoria 3003

THOMAS NELSON AND SONS (CANADA) LTD
81 Curlew Drive Don Mills Ontario

THOMAS NELSON (NIGERIA) LTD
8 Ilupeju Bypass PMB 21303 Ikeja Lagos

Tenth Impression 1979
0 17 424304 9

Printed in Hong Kong

Contents

CONTENTS

PART TWO: THE SCHEMES OF WORK

Introduction

Aim

The aim of these books on handwriting is to show how children may be taught to acquire from an early age a fluent, legible style of handwriting, which will not only serve their everyday needs in school, but will also meet the demands of later life for a speedy, legible and graceful style of writing.

Handwriting is essentially a tool subject. Its prime function is to meet the needs of all other subjects. Its essential qualities are legibility and fluency; they are of equal importance, and only when they are taught together does writing stay taught.

Handwriting is also, however, the most universal of all crafts and must be judged by aesthetic as well as utilitarian standards.

Style

The simple letter forms learned in the infant classes are prototypes of the traditional and satisfying forms employed by the Renaissance scribes. They are developed continuously, with only minor modifications, throughout the infant and primary stages. They are easy to teach and are easily learned by all children whatever their level of ability, and if taught by the methods suggested, do not readily become illegible even when written at considerable speed. When written with a square-edged pen in the later primary stages, an extremely pleasing, modern, Italic hand is produced.

No attempt is made to join all letters in words. Ligatures are used only where they come naturally and easily. Unnecessary ligatures, loops and flourishes merely impair legibility, do not add to the fluency and rhythm of writing and their use is therefore discouraged.

Method

The teaching of handwriting is largely the teaching of movements. In the skilled writer, these movements are produced speedily, rhythmically and almost wholly automatically. The teacher must, therefore, have a thorough knowledge of the mechanics of handwriting and be familiar with the psychological and pedagogical principles applicable to the teaching and learning of handwriting movements if her efforts are to be fully effective. The methods detailed in this scheme are based on recent research and classroom experience.

The teacher will find many opportunities for the incidental teaching of handwriting when children are writing in the service of other class subjects. In general, however, most of the intensive formal instruction should be attempted in short daily lessons on handwriting.

Of necessity, the schemes of work in this book are largely, and the work books almost wholly, devoted to the work to be undertaken during these short periods of formal instruction.

Part One

The General Theory

Summary of Work in the Primary Classes

In the infant rooms the pupils should have learned to make the prototype letter forms speedily and rhythmically, well-shaped and where possible in one smooth continuous movement. They will be accustomed to writing stories and exercises with considerable fluency and rhythm in unjoined script. Although they have received no formal instruction in ligaturing letters in words, pupils who are writing at speed with ease and freedom will already be attempting to join letters together.

After any necessary brief revision and consolidation of the work of the infant stage, formal instruction in the writing together of pairs and then groups of letters is begun. The principles governing the ligaturing of letters and the appropriate teaching methods are described in detail on page 21 and in the relevant portions of the scheme of work for each class. It must be stressed that the teacher's task is not to teach pupils how to join letters in words, but how to write together groups of letters speedily, rhythmically and legibly.

By the middle of the second year in a primary class, the formal instruction in ligaturing will have been completed.

In the third year, pupils begin to learn to write with pen and ink. Initial instruction is based on the use of the rounded, unyielding, fountain-pen type of pen-point which gives unshaded writing. In the latter part of the fourth year all instruction in writing with pen and ink is based on the use of the square-edged pen to give shaded writing. The scheme can, however, be readily modified to introduce the use of the square-edged pen at an earlier or later stage as desired.

The progress made by individual children will vary widely and uniformity of standard must not be expected nor demanded. The teacher must therefore be familiar with the whole scheme, and suit the instruction to the needs of the children.

Throughout each of the primary years, constant attention is paid to the basic writing techniques and to the writing of letters, words and sentences with increasing fluency and excellence of form. The methods of writing letters together, instructions regarding the spacing of letters, words, and lines of writing, the relative heights of letters and parallelism of writing strokes are revised briefly in each year.

It is not sufficient merely to be able to write excellent letter forms. If writing is to serve its prime purpose as a tool subject, the children must also learn to write with considerable fluency. This can only be achieved by much practice in writing speedily and rhythmically at all stages. Rhythmic exercises and pattern-making exercises are given at all stages to help the child to learn to manipulate his writing instrument with the necessary dexterity and rhythm, and to assist in the development of the speed, ease and general excellence of his writing.

Methods by which the child, as well as the teacher, may check and assess the standard of achievement in writing, are given. It is necessary to make regular checks on both the speed and the quality of the writing produced. It is also an essential part of the teacher's task to ensure that practice in writing is of the right kind and is adequately motivated. Children will make most progress when they are consciously striving to improve their performance and if they have been stimulated to take a pride in writing fluently and well.

Basic Principles, Techniques and Methods

Learning to write

In learning to write, a child has to acquire a unified motor habit for each letter, and in later stages for combinations of letters, so that the movements required to reproduce letters or combinations are subject to the minimum of visual or conscious control. These motor habits are acquired principally by intensive practice which must be effectively directed and adequately motivated. In the infant room, and to a lesser extent in the primary stages, the use of apparatus and methods which provide kinaesthetic sensations leads more readily to the establishment of the required habits. Such apparatus and methods are described in detail in the Infant Teacher's Book and are referred to where relevant in this book.

The child must also acquire as habits: a satisfactory method of sitting at his desk; the correct method of holding and using the writing instrument; and muscular relaxation when writing. The teacher must, therefore, give constant attention to these aspects of the instruction. If the child is to learn to write fluently, he must be given much practice in doing so. Although on occasions the pupil may benefit from writing fairly slowly and carefully with close visual attention to the form of the characters being written, this should be the exception rather than the rule and even this form of writing must be done rhythmically and freely. However, children should never be expected to write at such a speed beyond their natural reactive rate that grave deterioration of letters takes place.

Formal and informal instruction

Children learn to write more readily when what they write is satisfying, interesting and has some obvious purpose for them. In general, their writing in the service of ordinary class work meets these requirements and most of their practice in writing will be done at these times. Many opportunities will occur during these periods for correcting faulty techniques, for observing and assessing the quality and fluency of writing and for determining what remedial or new instruction is required. Reasonably neat and tidy work must always be demanded. During these informal times of writing, children should put into practice the lessons they have learned during the more formal periods of instruction. In a sense, therefore, each time the child writes is a lesson in handwriting.

If, however, handwriting is to serve its prime function as an essential tool of learning, it must at all ages be serviceable to the point that the child is able to think and write at the same time. If he is to write happily, rejoicing in his ability to tell a story and to devote his whole attention to the ideas he wishes to express, he must not be expected to pay more than a bare minimum of attention to the writing process itself, nor must he be subject to frequent interruption and instruction by the teacher.

Basic handwriting instruction must therefore receive attention at other times. This scheme is based on the assumption that there will be short, frequent, formal writing lessons in which the pupil receives intensive instruction in the fundamentals of handwriting and has the opportunity to learn and practise new techniques. A daily period of about ten minutes duration will be found to be effective. Normally, during each of these periods, only one very limited aspect of the work, such as learning how to write a particular group of letters or a special kind of ligature, should be covered. It is an essential part of the teacher's task to make these formal periods of instruction interesting and meaningful to the child, who should not only know precisely what he has to do, but why he is attempting to do it. He will delight in acquiring proficiency in the skill of writing if he understands its purpose, if he is expected to make use of his skill in his ordinary class work, and if he is able to measure his progress and compare his achievements with others in his class.

The Work Books in this scheme, which are almost wholly devoted to the work to be attempted during the periods of formal instruction will be of much help both to teacher and pupil.

Fluency

In terms of the function of handwriting, slow writing cannot be regarded as good writing. The main difference between the traditional and modern methods of teaching handwriting is probably the insistence on the child's ability to write with fluency and reasonable speed at all stages of instruction. This does not mean that the child must always be made to write at maximum speed nor that he should be pushed beyond his natural reactive rate. He will only learn to write speedily, yet legibly, when he is able to write fluently.

Fluent handwriting is handwriting which does virtually flow across the page and is produced smoothly and rhythmically. Fluency comes from response to rhythm which in turn comes from ease of movement. Children will only be able to write fluently and therefore speedily, without loss of legibility, if they are given much practice in doing so at all stages of instruction.

Much attention should be given to the mechanics of writing so that children are able to make easy flowing movements. Observation of the child and how he performs his work is at times more important than observation of the work he produces.

The slow, laboured copying of letters and words is not an effective method of teaching and is to be avoided. In the infant room the child must learn to write letters and numerals at a reasonable speed with an easy flowing movement. His unjoined writing must be performed in the same way, and it should be noted that this type of writing can be as speedy, fluent and rhythmical and therefore as essentially cursive as writing in which all the letters in words are joined. In the primary classes the pupil must continually strive to improve the fluency of his writing. It will be found that fluency is the aspect of writing which probably gives most satisfaction to the pupil and this satisfaction, of course, plays a large part in contributing to permanent learning.

Rhythmic pattern-making exercises such as those illustrated in the Work Books will help in the development of fluency. Exercises such as the following can be used with young pupils and developed in the later stages:

(1) Rhythmic patterns which progress across the page from left to right to the verse rhythm of simple rhymes:

Jack and Jill went up the hill
to fetch a pail of water;

Jack fell down and broke his crown,
and Jill came tumbling after.

Mary, Mary, quite contrary,
how does your garden grow?

With silver bells and cockle shells,
and pretty maids all in a row.

(2) Straight lines, ellipses, elements of letter forms and patterns performed (a) to the descriptive naming of movements—down up, down up, down up, etc. (b) to rhythmical counting (c) to music. When straight lines are used the count may be made on each stroke, both down and up:

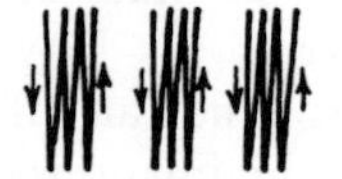

1–6 1–6 1–6
or
down up, *down up*, etc.

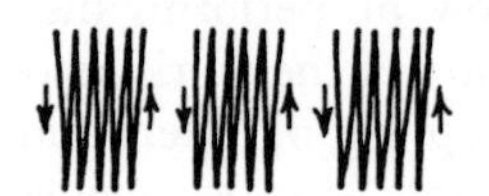

1–10 1–10 1–10
or
down up, *down up*, etc.

1,2 1,2 1,2 1,2 1,2 1,2 etc.
or
down up, *down up*, etc.

The exercises should be practised starting either with a down-stroke or an up-stroke and a steady rhythmical movement must be maintained.

With ellipses the same principle can be applied, either counting two (one for the down-stroke and one for the up-stroke), or counting one for the complete ellipse. They should be practised with a clockwise as well as an anti-clockwise movement:

1,2 1,2 1,2 for each elipse or *down up, down up*, etc.

1–10 1–10 1–10
Complete elipse to each count of one, or *down and down*, etc.

When these exercises are first attempted, the establishment of correct rhythmical movement rather than precision or excellence of form must be the first objective. Before the child writes on paper, he should learn the movement and establish rhythm in making it by sliding the blunt end of his pencil over the paper or by keeping the point of his pencil just off the surface of the paper. When he is familiar with the movement, the point of the pencil can be lowered and the exercise begun with a ' running start '.

Each of the exercises shown above should be used very frequently in every primary class. No useful indication of speeds can be given as it will be found that variation of speed is very great even for children in the same class. Neither great speed nor excellence of form should be sought at the expense of rhythmical movement.

The Work Books contain many exercises for the development of rhythmical movement, such as the following :

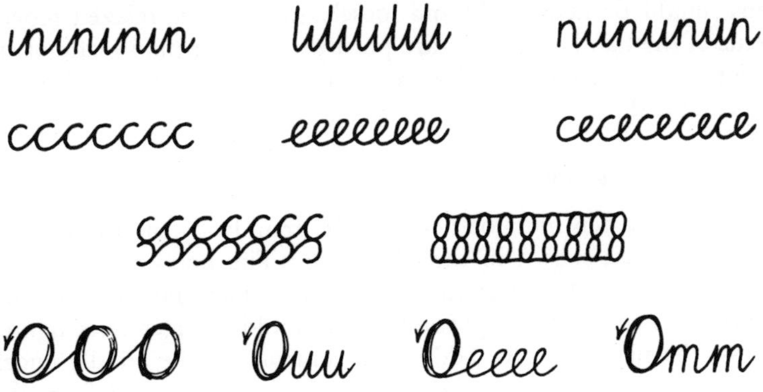

Posture

The child must be comfortably seated at a desk of the correct height in such a way that the writing hand and arm have unrestricted movement. The teacher who does not attend to this seemingly obvious and elementary requirement handicaps her pupils and nullifies much of her instruction.

Lighting should be from the left-hand side. There is an advantage in using a desk with a slight slope, but this is a disadvantage for most other subjects, especially in the infant room.

The desk and seat should be of such a height that when the pupil is seated as shown in the diagrams, the top of the desk is level with the lower ribs, the thighs are horizontal and the feet can be placed flat on the floor. The elbows should project a short distance over the edge of the desk which acts as a fulcrum for the forearm. The arms should be held easily and loosely so that free relaxed movements of the hands and arms are possible. Young pupils cannot sit for long in one position and a fixed and rigid posture should never be demanded.

Holding a pencil or pen

The pencil or pen must be held lightly, mainly by the thumb and index finger, as shown in the diagrams. The body of the pencil rests near the basal joint of the index finger, which should be slightly curved. The tip or top portion of the middle finger rests lightly against the pencil to give additional control. If the middle finger presses too firmly against the pencil and usurps control from the index finger, the movement of the pencil will be impaired. The last two fingers of the right hand may either rest lightly on the paper or be tucked comfortably out of the way. The ball of the hand may rest on the paper, but so lightly that the hand can progress easily across the page.

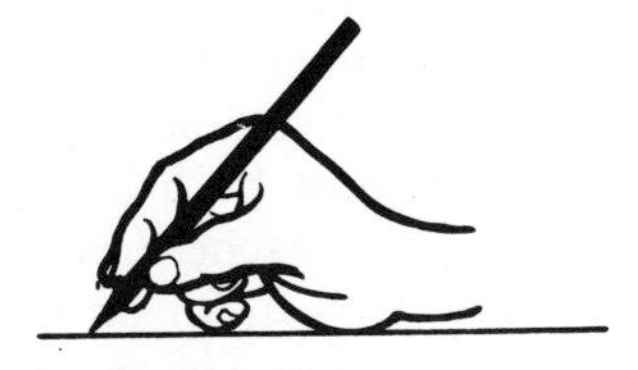

The pencil should lie at an angle of about 45° to the plane of the paper and should point along the line of the forearm to the right of the shoulder.

It is possible to write by keeping the hand and arm immobile and flexing the fingers only, by immobilising the fingers and moving the hand only, or by keeping the fingers and hand in a fixed position and moving the pencil by extensions, retractions and turning of the forearm. The method adopted depends to a certain extent on the style of handwriting to be used.

All the above methods are in current use with a fair measure of success. It will be found, however, that the pencil will move most easily and smoothly on the paper if the hand, fingers, wrist and arm are relaxed, and if the movement of the pencil is achieved by almost imperceptible movements of fingers and hand and by extensions and retractions of the hand from the wrist.

If a child already holds the pencil in some wrong manner it will be extremely difficult to break him of the habit. He will complain that the new grip feels strange and uncomfortable and that he cannot write well, as indeed he will not when he first holds the pencil in this way.

A change to the correct method of holding and using a pencil will be of ultimate benefit to the writer, but the conversion period may prove to be a trying time for both pupil and teacher, and it must be left to the discretion of the teacher to determine what adjustments should be made by individual children. When a child is required to change his method of holding or using a pencil, he should be given considerable practice in making the scribbling movements and patterns illustrated on the early pages of the Work Books. Only after he has gained confidence in using the pencil in the new way and no longer feels the new hold strange and uncomfortable should he be allowed to practise writing letters and words.

No matter how a pencil is held there are two fundamental rules which must be observed. First of all, it must be held *lightly*—so lightly that it can very easily be pulled by the teacher from between the child's fingers; and secondly, it must press *lightly* on the paper so that it can move speedily and with complete ease in any direction.

What has been said regarding the method of holding and using a pencil is equally applicable to the use of a pen. Indeed, since a pencil can be used with fair success no matter how it is held, while a pen must be held in a reasonably correct manner if writing is to be produced with ease and speed, there is some justification for introducing pupils to the use of a pen at an early age, in order to convert them to the correct use of a pencil.

Arm movements

As a line of writing progresses across the page the hand and arm holding the pencil must move from left to right. This can be done either by moving the whole arm sideways as in *figure 1*, or by moving the hand in an arc with its centre at a point in front of the elbow as shown in *figure 2*. The arm rests with the large muscle of the forearm on the edge of the desk and pivots about this point.

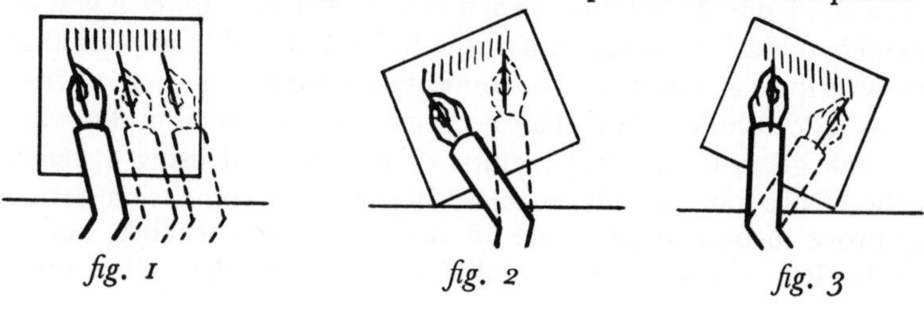

fig. 1 *fig. 2* *fig. 3*

The first method is easier for young children and enables vertical pulled strokes towards the centre of the body to be made easily. The paper should be placed with its bottom edge parallel to the edge of the desk and slightly to the right of the centre of the body. Writing produced in this way will tend to be vertical.

The second method should be used with older pupils as it facilitates the unrestricted speedy movement of the pencil across the page. In this case the pencil moves in a line which is slightly curved and inclined to the edge of the desk. If the page is wide both forms of movement may have to be used. When the second method is used the paper should be placed a little to the right of the centre of the body and tilted slightly in the way shown so that the pencil moves in a path as nearly parallel as possible to the top edge of the paper. When the paper is tilted in this way the pulled strokes to the centre of the body will slope to the right as shown and sloping writing will be produced.

For a left-handed writer the paper should be placed slightly to the left of the centre of the body and tilted in the opposite direction. In this case the pulled strokes will tend to slope backwards, but in the case of left-handed writers this should be tolerated. (*See fig. 3*)

If a right-handed pupil writes with a backward slope it is because his posture is faulty or he has turned his hand inward, so pulling the pencil diagonally across the body instead of directly towards it. Pupils should not be allowed to write in this inefficient manner.

Relaxation

Free, rhythmic and speedy writing movements are inhibited by tensed muscles and such tension results in the early onset of cramp and fatigue. Unfortunately the desire of the child to write well, to please the teacher, or the consciousness of having to hold the pencil or write in a particular way may induce undesired tension. Formal instructions given to the child on the necessity of relaxing or on how to do so may achieve the opposite effect to that intended.

Children should be introduced to relaxation exercises such as those listed below and should practise them before they are required to use them during a writing lesson. When they are familiar with the exercises and are aware of their purpose, they should be encouraged to use them on each occasion they write, both before and during a spell of writing.

RELAXATION EXERCISES

(1) Sit in writing position with arms dangling limply. Let hands flutter loosely.

(2) Lay forearms limply on the desk in the correct writing position. Raise and lower the elbows several times. Raise the forearms slightly with the desk edge serving as an axis, the hands hanging loosely and the finger-tips touching the desk.

(3) Place elbows on the desk with the forearms held upright. Let the hands flap loosely backwards and forwards while the fingers make slight snatching movements.

(4) Clench and unclench the fist repeatedly with the fingers spread.

(5) Drum lightly with fingers—' piano playing.'

(6) Circle hands inwards and outwards, then fling loosely sideways and downwards.

Practice

In the learning of any complex motor-skill such as handwriting, typing or piano playing, improvement comes in stages. The learning curve rises regularly and then levels off. This is followed by further rises and plateaux. These plateaux may be regarded as breathing spaces wherein muscular co-ordination has reached the psychological limit. Further progress cannot be made because the neuromuscular organisation of the performer is for the time being incapable of greater achievement. It may be so incapable for purely physical reasons, but more generally the limitation comes from lack of knowledge as to how the improvement may be achieved, from misdirected effort due to misunderstanding of the nature of the difficulty, from relaxation of attention and desire to improve, or from conflicting methods of practice. The standard of performance may even decrease for a time as new knowledge and methods are acquired and are integrated with what was previously known and done.

The rise from one plateau to another representing a higher level of achievement generally comes from a change of method. It comes when the mind grasps the significance of short cuts and of a better method of performance.

Improvement in handwriting can come, however, only if the writer is consciously striving to improve and if he is shown by the teacher how he may improve his performance. Practice alone does not make perfect. Only adequately motivated and properly directed practice will lead to worth-while improvement. The wrong kind of practice such as the routine production of pages of transcription without supervision from the teacher may result in the performance being consolidated at an extremely low level. The longer a pupil practises at one level of achievement without making efforts to improve, the more firmly will his performance become established at that level and the more difficult will it be for him to become a better writer.

Improvement in a skill is unlikely to take place unless there is some standard for measuring the level of performance. If the speed of writing as well as its quality is measured or compared with a standard or with a previous performance, the writer will benefit greatly from the knowledge. The process of learning a skill is generally enjoyed when the skill is useful and if improvement in performance is evident. The feelings that accompany the acquisition of a skill play a big part in improving the level of performance.

The teacher must make full use of these facts if the teaching is to be effective. In brief:

(1) Pupils should feel that it is important and worth while to try to improve their writing and they should consciously strive to do so.

(2) Pupils must have a clear understanding of what they are expected to do to improve their writing. They should receive precise guidance as to the most effective methods of doing so.

(3) Practice must always be directed to the achievement of a clearly defined and specific objective, e.g. the writing of a pair of letters with increasing speed, rhythm and excellence of form.

(4) There must, therefore, be formal periods of specific instruction in writing as distinct from other times in school when the pupil's writing is done in the service of other subjects. Frequent short periods of practice are the most effective. It is better to have a ten-minute lesson each day than one of fifty minutes once a week.

(5) The lessons learned during the formal periods of instruction should in time be reflected in the writing produced by pupils during ordinary class work. Careless and untidy writing should never at any time be accepted by the teacher, though when a pupil is writing an exercise such as an essay, his attention should be devoted to the subject matter of the essay rather than to the improvement of his handwriting.

(6) The teacher must make frequent checks on the speed and quality of the writing produced by the pupils. Instructions on how to do so are contained in the scheme of work for each class and in the pupil's Work Books. The children also must learn how to make these tests and comparisons.

(7) Improvement in performance will be retarded no matter how hard a pupil strives if his writing techniques are faulty. The teacher must pay constant attention to posture, the way in which the pencil is held, how it is manipulated and how the pupil attempts to carry out instructions. It is often much more important to watch the writer than to watch what is written.

Patterns and scribbling exercises

Scribbling exercises such as those illustrated at the beginning of the first two Primary Work Books give the pupil the opportunity of learning to hold and manipulate his pencil or pen correctly before he attempts to write letter forms. They help to increase his dexterity with a pencil, and exercise and loosen the muscles used in writing. These exercises can be practised by pupils at any time on scrap paper, over an old page of writing, or even on newsprint if a soft black pencil is used. Exercises of this type are useful if performed with speed and rhythm immediately before a pupil begins a formal writing exercise.

Patterns made from rows and combinations of letters are also useful for giving practice in using the writing instrument and in writing the letter forms used in the pattern. Children should be given opportunities to write patterns such as those illustrated throughout the Work Books, and to devise patterns for themselves. They will derive considerable pleasure from doing so, especially if coloured pencils are used, and if they can use these patterns and borders for decorating notices, posters, pages of writing or greetings cards.

Care must, however, be exercised in the use of these patterns. It is easy for deterioration of letter forms and ligatures to take place and to pass unnoticed in a complicated pattern. The prime function of these patterns must always be to add variety to practice in writing letter forms quickly and well.

The Left-handed Writer

The left-handed writer has to overcome many difficulties unknown to the right-handed child, but there is no reason why he should not learn to write well with considerable fluency if shown how to do so. Free writing movements are restricted since the writing arm instead of moving away from the body has to move towards and across it. The left hand hides what is being written and tends to smudge ink-writing since the hand must pass over what has been already written. Ligatures have to be made with a push-stroke instead of a 'sidled' one, and if the pen point is finely pointed or flexible, it will tend to dig into the paper and splutter. To add to the difficulties of the left-handed pupil, the inkwell will be at the wrong side of the desk, and blots may result from carrying the pen across the exercise book.

No attempt should be made to effect a change of hand in pupils in whom left-handed dominance is already established. Such pupils must be shown how to overcome some of their difficulties.

(1) Grossly unorthodox postures should not be permitted, but the body may be turned slightly to the right to allow the left arm greater freedom of movement.

(2) The pencil or pen should be held slightly farther away from the point than is usual to enable the pupil to see what is being written and to avoid the hand smudging the writing.

(3) The paper may be placed slightly to the left of the pupil and may slope slightly downwards to the right.

(4) The pencil should be held so that it points along the left forearm. There is no need for the hand to be turned inwards so that the end of the pencil points away from the body.

(5) A fountain pen with a smooth, rounded, unyielding type of nib will be found easier to use than a finely pointed dip pen. If shaded writing is desired a reverse oblique nib should be used.

(6) Since pushed-strokes are difficult for left-handed writers, they will find that the absence of loops and long ligatures in the style of writing used in this scheme is to their advantage.

Letters and Numerals

The highly formalised prototype letters learned in the infant room are used with only minor modifications at all later stages. These elementary letter forms which consist mainly of vertical strokes and ellipses are made, where the structure permits, in one smooth, continuous and rhythmical movement.

As the skill of the writer and the speed of his writing develop, minor changes of the elementary letter forms will take place naturally. In particular, downstrokes and the major axis of the elliptical bodies of letters will tend to slope slightly to the right. Individual variations of style will develop, but this should not be discouraged if the letters are of good form and preserve their essential characteristics. The child should not be expected to make reproductions by consistently slow and painstaking copying of the somewhat colourless basic letter forms which are illustrated. These are merely the prototypes from which each child will develop his own characteristic letter forms. The child's letter forms should be written with such speed, ease and rhythm that they exhibit a grace and liveliness lacking in the prototypes.

It will be noted that there is a complete absence of the loops which are characteristic of the English Round Hand style of writing. The reason for this is explained in the section dealing with ligatures.

The basic letter forms used at the different stages are illustrated on the following pages.

LETTER FORMS USED IN THE SCHEME

Column 1 Prototype forms used in infant classes
Column 2 Prototype forms used in primary classes
Column 3 Final form in primary classes—filiform
Column 4 Final form in primary classes—shaded

a	a	a	a	n	n	n	n
b	b	b	b	o	o	o	o
c	c	c	c	p	p	p	p
d	d	d	d	q	q	q	q
e	e	e	e	r	r	r	r
f	f	f	f	s	s	s	s
g	g	g	g	t	t	t	t
h	h	h	h	u	u	u	u
i	i	i	i	v	v	v	v
j	j	j	j	w	w	w	w
k	k	k	k	x	x	x	x
l	l	l	l	y	y	y	y
m	m	m	m	z	z	z	z

PROTOTYPE LETTER FORMS USED IN PRIMARY CLASSES

The starting-point of each letter is shown by a cross and the method of writing by arrows.

Pulled-strokes are used in preference to pushed-strokes.
All letters other than f, i, j, t, and x, are written with one continuous, rhythmical movement.
The bodies of the letters a, b, c, d, g, o, p and q are oval or elliptical.

Relative Size of Letters

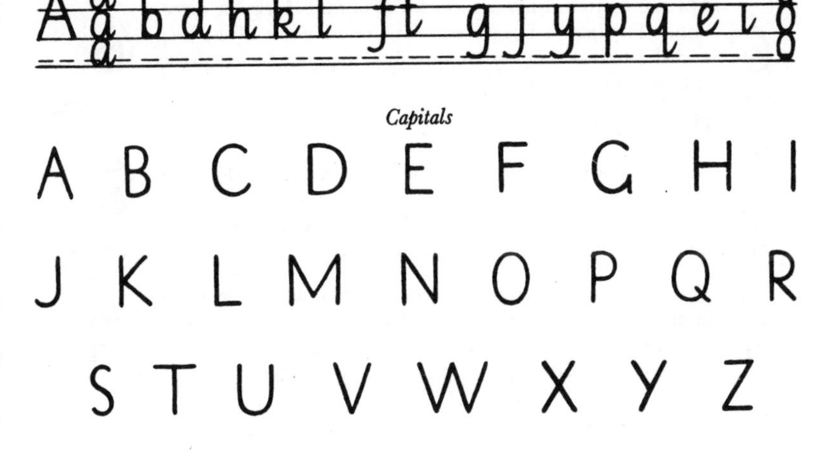

PROTOTYPES FOR USE IN TEACHING NUMERALS

The prototypes illustrated below are based mainly on the recommendations made in the report by the Scottish Council for Research in Education on the teaching of numerals.* They have been chosen from many possible varying forms so as to emphasise the essential form of each numeral as revealed by its history, for their stability, for their distinctiveness and so that they may not readily be confused with other numerals. All the numerals are the same size.

Method of Construction

0 Oval—not circular

1 Simple vertical stroke

2 Single curve and straight base. The distinctive element is the turn—not the head or stem.

3 The central turn is the emphatic element. The upper curve is slightly smaller than the lower.

4 The proportion of the parts is relatively unimportant if the cross stroke is made boldly and crosses the horizontal.

5 May be written with a horizontal attached flag or a detached flag at an angle of 45°.

6 May be written either in a clockwise or anti-clockwise direction. The loop is not closed. The relative size of the loop and the terminal curve are of minor importance as long as extremes are avoided.

7 Flat top and angular turn.

8 May be written by starting at the top with an anti-clockwise motion, or by beginning with a right-to-left downstroke. The latter method is better for a number of reasons. The top of the number may be left unclosed. (8 or 8)

9 The printed form of this numeral if written with a clockwise motion has certain advantages. The form illustrated here is more commonly used and is probably preferable, if it is learned and written in one continuous movement.

* *The Writing of Arabic Numerals*, by Dr G. G. Neill Wright, University of London Press Ltd., 1955

Ligatures

Ligatures between letters are justified only if they increase the speed and rhythm of writing without detracting seriously from the legibility. An unjoined or partly joined script may come to be written in time with considerable speed and rhythm and its legibility is likely to be very high. Ligatures of any kind are almost certain to detract in some measure from the legibility of writing. The teaching of them, especially if they involve loops, adds considerably to the teacher's task. It is difficult, however, to lift the pencil for the very short distance between the end of some letters and the beginning of the next. If in such a case the first letter ends in a movement which passes easily and naturally into the movement which makes the next letter, then the ligature is usually justified. Ligaturing is not simply a case of joining or not joining certain letters, but of ensuring a continuity of rhythmic movement.

Ligatures involving loops on ascenders and descenders are not used in this scheme. For a skilled writer, the loops characteristic of English Round Hand and its derived system may aid the rhythm of writing but they are not essential for the attainment of rhythm. The teaching and learning of them is a major burden to both teacher and pupil, and they are undoubtedly the chief cause of untidy and unsatisfactory writing. It can easily be shown that they do not add to the speed of writing and that they detract from legibility.

In this scheme, letters have been classified into groups for ease of reference when dealing with the writing together of letters.

The letters of Group 1, *a*, *c*, *d*, *e*, *h*, *i*, *k*, *l*, *m*, *n*, *t*, *u*, can readily be terminated with an incipient ligature consisting of a short upward flick of the pencil in the direction of the beginning of the next letter.

At the beginning of the primary stage, pupils terminate Group 1 letters in this manner. They then learn to carry this upstroke to the beginning of the letters of Group 2, *e*, *i*, *j*, *m*, *n*, *p*, *r*, *u*, *v*, *w*, *x*, *y*.

By the end of the first primary year they have learned to write together with considerable speed and as rhythmic wholes the common combinations of Group 1 to Group 2 letters and words containing these combinations.

Group 1 letters are not joined to the top of Group 3 letters, *b*, *f*, *h*, *k*, *l*, *t* (ascenders), although in the late primary classes when the pupil is sufficiently skilled and practised in writing at speed, there is scarcely any pencil lift between a Group 1 and Group 3 letter.

The letters of Group 4, *a*, *c*, *d*, *g*, *o*, *q*, *s*, likewise do not have a join from a Group 1 letter in the early stages.

The writing of Group 1 to Group 3 and Group 4 letters is treated in detail in the appropriate sections of the scheme of work for each class.

The letters of Group 5, *f*, *o*, *v*, *w*, can readily be ligatured to some letters which follow them in a word by means of a short stroke. This type of join is first taught in the second primary class.

The Group 6 letters, *b*, *g*, *j*, *p*, *q*, *s*, *x*, *y*, *z*, do not join easily or naturally to a following letter and no useful purpose is served in attempting to effect such joins.

The special difficulties which occur with the letters *e* and *r* are dealt with in detail in the appropriate section of the scheme of work for each class.

It must again be emphasised that the teacher's task is not to show how letters in words may be joined together, but how the successive movements which make a word are fused into a single rhythmic whole.

Writing with Pen and Ink

Handwriting is not generally taught in secondary schools and the pupils are normally expected to become proficient in the use of pen and ink before they leave the primary school.

WRITING WITH PEN AND INK

In this scheme, work with pen and ink is begun in the third primary class. A pen with a hard, smooth, unyielding point which produces unshaded writing is suggested for the early stages. This is followed by the use of a square-edged pen which produces shaded writing.

Before the scheme which is suggested is adopted or modified, the teacher or headmaster must first determine what his purpose is in teaching pupils to use pen and ink.

The aim of this handwriting scheme is to teach pupils to write speedily and well from an early age with the minimum of conscious attention to the mechanics of writing, so that undivided concentration may be given to the subject matter of the lesson which is being written. Neither the teaching and learning of a subject nor the development of skill in writing should be allowed to suffer from the premature insistence on the use of pen and ink for written exercises.

Pupils can be, and are in many schools, taught to use pen and ink from an early age, and to produce formal shaded writing of great beauty. This can only be done at the expense of the speed of writing and of its full usefulness in the service of other subjects. The headmaster must decide for himself the extent to which in the early stages writing is to be regarded primarily as an art form, a utilitarian tool subject or a combination of both.

In the later stages of instruction this question does not arise, for pupils who have learned to write in pencil with considerable ease and fluency have no difficulty in using a pen with almost equal facility from the start. Letter forms used for pencil-work, when written easily and rhythmically with a square-edged pen, have a grace and beauty lacking in writing which has been acquired by a process of slow and laborious copying of shapes.

The fountain pen with a hard, rounded, unyielding point which moves easily over the paper in any direction is the modern writing instrument *par excellence*. Pupils who have learned to use a pencil correctly will need little further instruction in writing with this type of pen.

Like a pencil, this fountain pen produces writing of fairly uniform thickness. While this type of writing is easier to produce and meets the needs of the school better than shaded writing, it is undoubtedly insipid. It would be a great pity if pupils were to regard writing merely as a convenient tool and fail to learn that it is also a form of art and a means of self-expression. Shaded writing can be a thing of great beauty and all but the least able pupils should be given the opportunity of learning how to improve the quality and appearance of their writing by this means.

If shaded writing is desired, a square-edged pen should be used in preference to a finely-pointed, flexible and almost inevitably scratchy pen point. The square-edged pen produces the gradation of line in a natural way according to the movements of the pen. The flexible-pointed pen produces variation of thickness by alteration of pressure on the point. These alterations of pressure are not natural reactions and are almost impossible to produce correctly when writing at speed.

Fountain pens of reasonable quality have many advantages over dip pens and will probably replace them in schools as they have already done elsewhere. They are available at a reasonable cost with easily replaceable points of either the rounded or square-edged type, in all widths.

Materials

Paper and exercise books

Most of the practice in writing letters and words during formal lessons should be done on loose sheets of cheap paper. If pupils are to have the requisite amount of practice a considerable amount of paper will be used and an ordinary exercise book would soon be filled with material which ought not to be preserved.

For work with pencil, paper such as blank newsprint will be quite satisfactory. If a soft black pencil is used much of the writing of scribbling exercises, pattern making, letters, joins and even words can be done over newsprint or on used pages of old exercise books. An exercise book should normally be used towards the end of a lesson or group of lessons when pupils have already had much practice in the exercise which is to be written in the book. The main function of the exercise book will be to give pupils final practice and to record their achievement and progress at each stage of instruction, but it is *not* intended to be a book kept for work written slowly and carefully. If the teacher feels it is necessary for pupils to have a book in immaculate condition for show purposes, a second exercise book should be kept and used only very occasionally for this purpose.

When the pupil begins to write with ink, paper of a much better quality will be required. A square-edged pen demands paper of a very good quality. As with pencil work, the bulk of the practice with pen should be done on loose sheets of paper.

Ruled or blank paper

Blank paper facilitates writing suited to the child's particular stage of motor-muscular development and he should not be restricted by having to write on or between lines. To restrict freedom of movement or size of letters, at least in the early stages, will have an adverse effect on the development of a fluent hand. The majority of children will readily adopt the size of writing suggested by the teacher and only excessively small or large letters should be disallowed.

Lines are a comfort to the teacher as they give a specious appearance of tidiness and quality to a pupil's handwriting. They are, however, an impediment to the development of the child's ability to write freely well-proportioned letters. If children are obliged to write continually between lines, they will take longer than necessary to appreciate the relative size of letters and may even develop faulty letters by attempting to conform to the rulings on the page.

Children very quickly learn to write straight across the page and to space lines a reasonable distance apart if they are given practice in doing so. If a line of writing produced by a child is not horizontal the cure is to correct his posture and not to force him to write between ruled lines.

Pencils and pens

Children will continue to use pencils for writing throughout the primary classes. Even when they learn to use pen and ink, some of the formal practice in writing, as well as most of their written work in other subjects, will continue to be done in pencil. One of the disadvantages of a pencil is that it is possible to write with it no matter how it is held. Unless the teacher pays considerable attention to the correct method of holding a pencil, not only will the pupil be unable to use the pencil to the best advantage, but he may acquire a writing habit which is almost impossible to unlearn when he has to hold a pen in the correct manner.

It is not easy for a young child to hold a narrow pencil lightly yet firmly enough to give adequate control. The use of a plastic holder about 12 cm long and about 1 cm outside diameter increases the area of gripping surface and overcomes this difficulty, and also enables the child to use a pencil stub without distortion of the correct hold.

For the same reason a dip-pen with a very narrow holder should not be used. Penholders of about the same width at the finger-hold as a fountain pen are preferable.

Ball-point, Biro-type pens are now widely used by adults instead of fountain pens because of their relative cheapness and convenience. Many children will use no other writing instrument during their adult lives and should accordingly have some instruction and practice in the use of this type of pen. The exercises of various types illustrated in the Work Books can be used for giving appropriate practice.

The ball-point pen does have certain disadvantages. It varies widely in quality. Certain types with a small diameter have to be held very firmly, pressed heavily on the paper and held at an unduly steep angle if they are to write well. The friction between the point of the pen and the paper is so slight that the point tends to skid almost uncontrollably over the surface resulting in the malformation of letters and the introduction of unnecessary and distorted ligatures. The writing produced by this type of pen is insipid and cannot be compared in quality or permanence with that produced by ink and a square-edged pen.

Not only does the writing produced by a ball-point pen tend to be bad itself but also the use of such a pen is detrimental to the development of good writing with an ordinary pen or pencil.

Ball-point pens of the cheaper variety do not produce a fine, clean, uniform line and are not generally successful when used for arithmetic or fine work. They have no advantages over the pencil for work in the infant or early stages of the primary school, and their use instead of fountain pens in secondary schools will depend on the type of work to be written, and the nature and amount of writing required by the children in later life.

Whether they make use of ball-point pens or not, all primary pupils should become proficient in the use of pen and ink.

Part Two

The Schemes of Work

Introduction

By the time a child reaches this stage he should have acquired a unified motor-habit for each letter and numeral. He should, in other words, be able to write each prototype letter and numeral rhythmically, speedily and well, even with the eyes closed, so that little conscious attention need be paid to individual letter forms or to the writing process during informal writing lessons. He should also have acquired the habit of sitting at his desk and of holding and using his pencil in such a way that the free and relaxed movements essential for good writing are possible. Constant attention must be paid to the basic writing techniques and remedial instruction should be given when required.

Since children vary considerably in ability and in the rate of their motor-muscular development, it is most unlikely that all pupils in a class will be at the same level of achievement. There may also be in the class children from other schools who have not learned to write the letters as patterns of movement or who have not had adequate training in correct posture, pencil usage and relaxation.

The teacher must therefore give individual instruction to pupils who have not acquired satisfactory writing techniques or who have not learned to write with the freedom, speed and excellence of letter form appropriate to the stage of instruction. Failure to do so can only result in faulty techniques and low levels of achievement becoming so firmly established with practice that further progress becomes almost impossible. It may be necessary in some cases to teach the class in sections with each group of children attempting work suited to the level of ability common to the group.

It follows from the above that the teacher must be familiar not merely with the content of the scheme for one particular class, but with the content, methods and techniques of the whole scheme, and more especially of the early stages.

Work Books

The four primary Work Books illustrate the work to be covered during the short daily periods of formal instruction in handwriting in each of the four primary classes. They contain only essential illustrations and a minimum of directions for the pupil. More detailed instructions and exercises have been placed in the Teacher's Book in the scheme of work for each class.

Each page of each Work Book contains approximately enough formal work for one week, but teachers may find it necessary to extend or condense the unit suggested to meet the particular needs of a class.

Each exercise should be performed by the children over and over again until they can write the particular letter combination or words both quickly and well. Only then should they attempt the next exercise.

Spiritmasters

These make provision for a rapid revision or remedial course in handwriting for pupils who have been unable to follow the complete primary scheme, or who have failed for some reason to achieve a satisfactory standard of handwriting by the later stages of the primary course.

These spiritmasters enable the teacher to duplicate the required number of worksheets providing instruction in all the salient parts of the Primary stages.

THE FIRST YEAR: WORK BOOK ONE

Summary

Formal instruction—10 minutes daily.

(1) Assessment of ability and achievement of pupils

(2) Left-handed writers (see page 15)

(3) Instruction in basic writing techniques

(4) Practice in writing well at speed all previously learned letters

(5) Writing Group 1 letters (see page 21) with incipient ligatures

(6) Joining Group 1 and Group 2 letters (see page 21)

(7) Writing words and sentences containing Group 1 and Group 2 combinations

(8) Practice in writing passages with considerable fluency.

(9) Testing speed and quality of writing

Informal instruction

The work detailed in this scheme and illustrated in Work Book 1 is the work which is to be undertaken during the short daily periods of formal teaching.

It is, however, essential that pupils have ample opportunity throughout the week for practising work covered during the formal lessons and that the progress made during these lessons should be reflected in the writing produced in the service of other subjects.

All writing must be done as fluently as possible. Attention must be paid to correct posture, pencil-hold and relaxation of muscles every time the child writes.

General

The stages in which the formal work for this year may be attempted are shown below. Each page of the Work Book corresponds approximately to the amount of formal instruction which can be covered in one week. The rate of progress, however, will depend on the ability and previous training of the pupils, and the teacher should feel free to modify the scheme to meet the requirements of individual pupils and on occasion to take lessons out of sequence.

Scheme of Work

Basic techniques — *Work Book, pages 1–3*

Ensure that each child is provided with a seat and desk suited to his stature so that it is possible for him to make free writing movements.

Observe each child carefully while written work is in progress. Note the general level of achievement of the class, and the stage of development of each child. Pay particular attention to the basic writing techniques.

Good posture, correct method of holding and using a pencil, relaxation of muscles while writing and the ability to write each of the prototype letters and numerals rhythmically, speedily and well are the foundations upon which the teacher is expected to build at this stage. Give individual, group or class instruction as required to improve these basic techniques, and give frequent attention to them during the year.

Discuss the pictures on pages 1 and 2 of the Work Book and refer to them throughout the year. It will not be possible to eradicate in a few weeks faulty habits of posture and pencil-hold which have developed over a long period of time. The teacher's task can be lightened if a routine for checking posture and pencil-hold is established and performed by each child every time he attempts to write—

(1) Am I sitting in the way shown in the picture?

(2) Am I holding my pencil correctly?

(3) Am I holding my pencil lightly?

(4) Are my muscles loose so that I can write quickly, lightly and easily?

It is probable that some pupils in attempting to sit correctly and hold the pencil in an unaccustomed manner may tense their muscles.

While instruction in the basic techniques is in progress pupils should be allowed considerable practice in scribbling, making patterns such as those illustrated on page 3 of the Work Book, and in writing quickly and easily letters already learned. This work can best be done on scrap paper. No new letter forms should be attempted at this stage, nor should too much attention be paid to the quality of the work produced.

Lower-case letters *Work Book, page 4*

Examine and discuss the letters shown on page 4 of the Work Book. The method of writing each letter, as far as possible in one smooth, continuous, speedy movement is shown. Attention should be drawn to any letter which is of a form different from that already learned. It will be seen that Group 1 letters are shown with incipient ligatures.

Pupils can be given an opportunity of writing all these letters, but no formal instruction or intensive practice in writing new letter forms should be attempted as this work is covered in detail in the succeeding lessons. They can, however, be given intensive practice in writing speedily and well the letters they already know.

The unjoined script used for written work in class should also be written with considerable fluency.

It should be noted that the children are not expected to make exact and immaculate reproductions of the prototype letter forms illustrated in the Work Books. They must have a clear conception of these forms, but they are not expected to make a reproduction as highly formalised as the model. These highly formalised prototypes are merely the central forms from which the efforts of each child will vary slightly. The letters written must of course be instantly and unmistakably recognisable, but they should have a liveliness and character which is lacking in the original model. On no account should the children be limited to slow, meticulous practice-writing in order to obtain an exact reproduction of the prototype letters.

Use cheap blank paper for practice in writing. Ruled paper is unnecessary at this or at any other stage of instruction and merely gives a specious appearance of tidiness at the expense of the pupil's ability to write with freedom and confidence.

Capitals and numerals *Work Book, page 5*

Follow the procedure outlined above for small letters. Refer to page 20 for reasons for using the forms of numerals shown.

Letters with incipient ligatures *Work Book, page 6*

The Group 1 letters

a c d e h i k l m n t u

should now be terminated by a short upward stroke as illustrated.

This incipient ligature consists merely of a short upward flick of the pencil in the direction of the beginning of the next letter. Care should be taken to ensure that this stroke is short, that it makes the correct angle with the preceding vertical line, and that the whole letter and flick are made in one continuous rhythmical movement:

l i n not l l l l l l n n

Since the spacing of the letters in a word depends on the angles made by the ligatures it is essential that the child learns to make the ligatures correctly:

him not him nor him

Discuss the letters *l* and *i* shown on page 6 of the Work Book. Illustrate on the blackboard the method of writing these letters and the correct angle and shape of the incipient ligature.

Give much practice in making the letters *l* and *i* with incipient ligatures. These letters should be written possibly several hundred times on scraps of paper or exercise books until the incipient ligatures can be made perfectly even when written at considerable speed. Allow the children to make patterns using these letters:

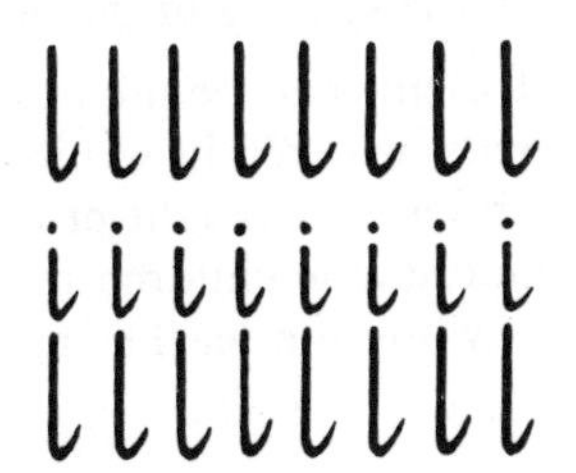

The rhythm of writing should not be broken by stopping to dot an *i*.

Do not forget that the whole purpose of pattern-making exercises is to give practice in making letters and ligatures correctly, speedily and rhythmically, and that the exercises can be definitely harmful unless the child strives to improve each successive letter or ligature. Mere mechanical practice in writing does not of itself lead to improvement.

The letters n, m and u *Work Book, page 7*

When the letters *l* and *i* can be written speedily and well show the children how to write *n*, *m* and *u*. The letter and ligature should be written speedily and rhythmically in one continuous movement.

The procedure outlined on page 7 of the Work Book should be followed:

(1) Trace over the outline of a large model with the blunt end of a pencil.

(2) Write a row of the letters carefully but not too slowly.

(3) Write several rows fairly quickly, striving to increase speed, rhythm and excellence of writing.

(4) When all the letters on the page have been taught, write words containing the letters taught to date:

in, pin, mine, nun, lump.

Each word should be written many times with increasing speed. Attention should be paid to the spacing of the letters.

(5) Pattern exercises, or variations of them, can be used to give additional practice in the movements involved in writing the letters. They may be used as each letter is taught or at the end of the group of lessons. The more able children may be employed in making such patterns while the teacher attends to those who need assistance.

The letters h, k and t — *Work Book, page 8*

Proceed as in the previous lessons. Draw attention to the relative heights of the letters and to the height of the cross-stroke on the letter *t*.

When the three letters can be written fluently and correctly, allow the children to practise writing words such as are illustrated in the Work Book, e.g. him, lit, tin, kit, hum, hunt, kilt, link, think, milk, hill. The letters in these words must be written with good incipient ligatures, but pupils should not be given instruction at this stage in joining letters in a word. Pattern exercises as before.

The letter o — *Work Book, page 9*

Adopt the procedure shown on page 9 of the Work Book for teaching the letter *o*. Give plenty of practice in the preliminary scribbling exercise to help establish a unified motor-habit for the other letters which have the letter *o* as their basic shape.

Note that the letter is not circular but elliptical and that although it has been illustrated with its main axis vertical, ideally this axis should incline slightly to the right. In time when the children are able to write with great ease and speed, the axis will incline naturally in this way. Ignore this refinement at this stage and spend much time in getting pupils to write this letter well, rhythmically and at considerable speed.

Test the class to find how many well-formed *o*'s each child can write in one minute.

Give pupils practice in writing words such as: no, to, on, oh, ton, hot, moon, look, hook, out, honk. Pattern exercises as before.

The letters c, a and d *Work Book, page 10*

Follow the procedure detailed on page 10 of the Work Book. Before each letter is written allow pupils to practise the continuous ellipse used as a preparatory exercise for the letter *o*. Emphasise that the letters *a* and *d* must each be made in one smooth, continuous movement. The pencil must not stop or be lifted from the paper between the start and finish of the letters. Words such as these may be practised: an, can, add, act, had, chat, did, dull, cut, duck, din.

The incipient ligatures must be made so that the spacing between letters is correct.

The letter e *Work Book, page 11*

Much practice must be given to *e* as it is the most frequently used letter and is not easy to make well at speed.

The following words can be used for practice: me, men, he, hen, den, end, each, teach, cell, tea, deal, keel, week, weak, deer, dear, heel, heal, leek, leak, heed, head, peal, peel, steel, steal, heap, eel.

Give much practice in making patterns using groups or rows of continuous *e*'s.

Letters with tails: g and q *Work Book, page 12*

Illustrate these letters on the blackboard. Show how a *g* can be made from an *o* and an *a*. Give practice in making a continuous *o* which is then extended to form a letter *g*.

Let the children trace over the letter illustrated on page 12 of the Work Book, then follow the usual procedure for teaching a letter. The tail of the *g* should be slightly less than the height of the body and it should not be too curly.

Teach the letter *q* in the same way as *g*. The tail of a *q* finishes with a very short upturned stroke.

Words for practice: go, ago, gun, log, leg, egg, dig, gone, game, good, gold, glue, glee, giant, queen, quake, queer, quite, quiet, quick, quilt, quit.

Letters with tails: f and j — *Work Book, page 13*

In the infant years a letter *f* without a tail will probably have been taught. Show how the new form may be developed from the old by adding a tail below the line.

Teach the letters *f* and *j* in the usual way in conjunction with the models in the Work Book. The tails of these letters should neither be too long nor have excessive curls:

f j not f j

Words for practice: of, off, foam, lift, fit, fig, fill, flit, float, flog, jam, jet, join, jig, jungle, joke, jaunt, juice, jolt, jag.

Letters with tails: p and y — *Work Book, page 14*

Demonstrate on the blackboard how the letter *p* is made in one continuous movement. Allow the children to practise making continuous clockwise ellipses, then follow the usual procedure in teaching the letter.

Words for practice: pup, peg, gap, puff, pipe, peel, flop, peep, puppet, apple, plump, pupil, pump, plug.

The cursive form of the letter *y* is used from now on. Show the children how to write this form instead of the straight line form which may have been in use so far.

Words for practice: you, yet, young, yell, yelp, yolk, joy, gay, jolly, poppy, jiffy, jelly.

The letters r, s, v, w, x and z *Work Book, page 15*

The remainder of the lower-case letters, *r*, *s*, *v*, *w*, *x* and *z*, which do not have incipient ligatures or descenders, should now be revised quickly. They are illustrated on page 15 of the Work Book. Note that *x* is the only one of these letters which is written with a lift of the pencil. Each letter should be written many times, at first fairly slowly and very well, and then at speed without undue deterioration of form. Give remedial instruction and further practice for letters which are badly made.

Practise words containing these letters: zip, buzz, zebra, six, vex, wax, view, waves, verse, screw, wire, extra, exit, box, axle, mix, fix, wives, drive, slaves, cows, foxes.

Before beginning the next section dealing with the joining of letters, revise the work which has been covered so far.

In particular, quickly revise the method of writing capital letters and numerals and give remedial instruction if necessary. Test the speed at which pupils write single letters and note the results for future reference.

Writing letters together *Work Book, page 16*

It should be remembered that the aim is not to join successive letters in a word but to ensure that the movement which goes to make one letter flows naturally into the movements which make the following letter, so that the two letters are written together easily and speedily as a continuous rhythmical whole.

The letters of Group 1, *a*, *c*, *d*, *e*, *h*, *i*, *k*, *l*, *m*, *n*, *t* and *u* end with incipient ligatures which can extend readily to the beginning of the letters of Group 2, *e*, *i*, *j*, *m*, *n*, *p*, *r*, *u*, *v*, *w* and *y*. The child has to learn not merely to join pairs of letters from these groups but to write the combinations in one smooth, continuous movement. A very large number of combinations of Group 1 and Group 2 letters is possible, but some combinations occur in the English language much more frequently than others.

Frequency of combinations of Group 1 to Group 2 letters:

(1) *Very frequently*—an en er he in

(2) *Frequently*—hi ar de ee le me ne te tr un ur

(3) *Fairly often*—ai ce di em ev ey ie iv ke li ly mi ni ti

(4) *Infrequently*—ae am ap au aw ay ci cr cu cy dr du dy ei ep eu ew hu hy im ip ir ki ln lu mu my nm nn tu ty ue um up nu ny

Since the combinations *an*, *en*, *er*, *he*, *in*, occur about forty times more frequently than those in the last group shown in the table above, it is reasonable that practice in the writing of a combination should be related to the frequency of its occurrence. Some combinations are, however, more difficult to write as rhythmical wholes than are others. Some children may find difficulty with combinations containing the letters *e* and *r*. Although in the lessons which follow and in the lessons set out in Work Book 4 an order is shown in which the combinations may be practised, the teacher should always ensure that individual pupils are given help and much practice with the combinations which prove to be difficult.

Writing the word 'in'

Demonstrate on the blackboard how the incipient ligatures from Group 1 letters may be carried on to the beginning of a Group 2 letter, thus making it possible to write two letters together without lifting the pencil from the paper.

Show by means of large letters on the blackboard how *in* may be written quickly in one continuous movement in this way. Allow the children to trace a number of times over the large example on page 16 of the Work Book. The word can also be traced many times on the desk with the finger or the blunt end of the pencil until a speedy, continuous rhythmical movement for the word has been mastered. The normal procedure should then be followed of allowing pupils to write a row of the words carefully, but smoothly and not too slowly. Make sure that each child adopts the correct posture and pencil-hold and is properly relaxed.

The children then proceed to write the combination very many times, gradually increasing speed as control develops, but ensuring that deterioration of letter forms and ligatures does not take place through trying to write too quickly at first. After sufficient practice they should be able to write this combination at least thirty-five times in a minute. The more able child should be able to write it more than fifty times in a minute. Combinations which are badly made do not count towards the total score. Speed tests may be taken for the writing of all combinations as they are learned. The teacher can use these tests to decide which children need more practice and whether the group or class can pass on to the learning of a new combination.

Joins to the letter i *Work Book, page 17*

Teach the writing of the combinations *li*, *hi*, *mi*, *ni* and *ti*, following the procedure detailed above. Each combination should be written many times, and only when one combination can be written fluently and correctly at a speed of about thirty-five times a minute should the next combination be practised.

When combinations of letters or words containing the letters *i* or *t* are being written the rhythm of the writing should not be broken by stopping to dot the *i* or cross the *t*.

Words for practice: him, hit, hill, hid, hip, his, lid, lie, lit, lip, nip, nib, mill, miss, mitt, tie, tin, till, tip, win, pin, bin, sin, din.

Unless the ligatures are made correctly the spacing of the letters in the word will not be correct.

Only one week has been allocated in this scheme to learning how to write the combination *in* and one week to joins to the letter *i*. Unless a very sound foundation has been laid in the infant department and in the earlier work for this class this time allocation will prove to be quite inadequate. It cannot be too strongly emphasised that very thorough grounding must be done at this stage. The teacher may therefore need to extend by another two or three weeks the time spent on these simple combinations.

Joins to the letter e — *Work Book, page 18*

It is not easy to make these joins well and extra time may have to be spent on joins to this letter.

Demonstrate on the blackboard and use the Work Book to show how joins such as *le*, *ne*, *he*, *ee* and *de* are made in one continuous movement.

The children should learn by the usual methods to write combinations such as *le*, *ne*, *he*, *ee*, *de*, *me*, *ke* and *ie*. Much practice should be given in learning to write these combinations speedily and well, and it may be necessary to spend more than one week on this unit, using the patterns and words on page 18 of the Work Book for further practice.

As combinations are successfully learned they may be integrated with the informal writing done in the course of ordinary class work, but the teacher must demand a high standard of neatness and care in all written work.

When the children are writing freely and quickly they will now tend to write all combinations of Group 1 and Group 2 letters as rhythmical wholes. Discourage all but the most able writers from attempting combinations which have not been taught and practised.

On no account should Group 1 letters be ligatured to Group 3 or Group 4 letters.

Joins from the letter e to Group 2 letters *Work Book, page 19*

Use the blackboard and page 19 of the Work Book to show how combinations such as *ei*, *en*, *em*, *er*, *ey*, *ev*, and *ew*, may be written in one speedy movement. The combinations *en* and *er* are very common and should receive particular attention.

Words for practice: hen, dew, her, few, eye, they, mend, deer, them, every, deep, pencil, dinner, clever, never, even, weigh, stew.

Joins to and from the letters m, n and u *Work Book, page 20*

These joins are so easily made that they afford an opportunity for demonstrating very clearly and precisely how letters may be written together. They also lend themselves to a lesson on the parallelism of up- and down-strokes. The exercises and the following words illustrated in the Work Book may be used for practice:

mum, nun, mug, gun, run, fun, sup, lump, fume, funny, penny, money, summer, drum, any, mine, mummy, tinny.

Joins from the letters a and c *Work Book, page 21*

These joins should not present much difficulty if the simpler combinations have been mastered. Practice should be given in writing the following combinations and words:

an, ai, ar, am, aw, ay, ce, cr, cu, cy, man, saw, say, map, air, can, nice, cup, cry, cell, ice, icy, fancy, face, cruel, circus, hay.

No attempt should be made to ligature to an *a* or a *c*.

Joins from d, h, k, l and t *Work Book, page 22*

The children will no doubt have already discovered that these letters join readily to Group 2 letters, but intensive practice should be given in writing together the combinations shown on page 22 of the Work

Book, i.e. *de*, *di*, *dr*, *du*, *he*, *hi*, *hu*, *ke*, *ki*, *le*, *lu*, *te*, *tr*, *ti*, *tu* and *ty*. Pay attention to the parallelism of all vertical strokes.

Words for practice: deep, dine, dry, dune, hero, him, hung, keen, king, lend, limp, luck, ten, tin, trip, turn, city.

Sentences such as those illustrated may be given for practice in writing with considerable fluency.

Letters which join and letters which do not join — *Work Book, page 23*

Revise joining Group 1 to Group 2 letters. Show the children why they should not attempt to join Group 1 letters to *a*, *c*, *d*, *g*, *o*, *q* and *s* which start in the one o'clock position. Such joins would result in unsightly loops at the tops of these letters as also would joins to the tops of ascenders such as *b*, *d*, *f*, *h*, *k*, *l* and *t*, which must not be attempted either:

as each hat tall

Give practice in writing words in which only some of the letters are joined, e.g. soup, gone, lump, rise, wasp, bee, fly, spider, beetle, ant, farmer, baker, doctor, teacher, rose, tulip, daisy, violet, lily, oak, elm, ash, beech, pine, birch. An occasional word in which all the letters are joined will be a help in learning to space letters correctly.

Writing quickly and well — *Work Book, pages 24 and 25*

Correct posture and pencil-hold and relaxed muscles are essential if writing is to be performed speedily and well. At no time should the quest for more speed be allowed to result in undesirable ligatures or gross deterioration of letter forms.

Children should have much practice in writing quickly on scraps of paper and they should be encouraged to practise at home. Exercises and words in which all the letters are joined, such as those shown on page 24 of the Work Book, will be found useful for this purpose. The scribbling exercises shown on page 3 should be used very frequently.

Words in which only some of the letters are joined, such as those shown on page 25 of the Work Book, should each be written many times as fluently as possible.

A standard form of speed test for this age of children is as follows: write 'Mary had a little lamb,' as often as possible in one minute. The number of letters—not words—written in one minute is the score.

In any class, the speed at which children write varies so very widely that norms for any given age cannot be laid down. Speeds between 15 and 100 letters per minute may well be obtained but an average of 50 letters per minute for a class at this stage is fairly common. Record the results obtained.

Sentences from the class reading book should now be written (a) very carefully but not too slowly; (b) at speed, without undue deterioration of letter forms or ligatures.

The relative size of letters *Work Book, page 26*

Use the diagram on page 26 of the Work Book to illustrate the relative size of the letters. The stems of ascenders and the tails of descenders are not quite as long as a small letter such as *a*. Children at this stage are unable to appreciate statements such as 'tall letters are not quite twice as big as the small letters', and they should be corrected only if they make stems or tails much longer or shorter than is desirable. If they constantly see good models of the correct proportions they will eventually be able to reproduce letters with the correct dimensions. Ruled paper will not help them to arrive more quickly at this stage of their development. Indeed, they are more likely to appreciate the subtle differences of the size and shape of letters if such differences are not masked by lines.

Spacing between words and lines

like a this ~ not this ~ nor this

At this stage there should be approximately the space of the letter *a* between successive words. A little more could be tolerated but not less. Ask the children to write a letter *a* with an incipient ligature between words they have written in their exercise books. It should fit in quite easily. Let them write a passage such as that shown on page 26 of the Work Book, and then let them examine what they have written to see if the spacing between words and lines is correct and if the letters are the right size and shape.

Writing neatly and well — *Work Book, page 27*

The children should write fairly slowly and carefully, but rhythmically, a passage such as that on page 27 of the Work Book. Let them then examine minutely what they have written and mark the following faults:

(a) badly written letters

(b) badly made ligatures

(c) faulty spacing between letters, words and lines

(d) faults in relative sizes of letters

(e) incorrect crossing of *f* and *t* and dotting of *i*

(f) bad alignment of lines

(g) lack of parallelism in vertical strokes.

Children should learn to look for these faults and to mark and correct passages they have written. It is a mistake to spend too much time writing passages very slowly and carefully. Such exercises should always be followed by writing the same passage fluently and correctly. At this stage the speedily written passage will almost certainly be inferior, but at a later stage the passage written with ease and speed will be much more satisfying.

Capital letters *Work Book, page 28*

Before revising the writing of all the capitals, as illustrated on page 5 of the Work Book, preliminary pattern-making exercises should be done mostly using straight lines. Eventually each letter should be written many times speedily and well. Additional practice in capitals may be had by writing boys' and girls' names such as those illustrated on page 28 of the Work Book.

Numerals *Work Book, page 29*

Revise the method of writing the numerals. Give plenty of practice in writing each numeral speedily but very well, and make speed tests. Numerals should also be written in rows and columns to give practice in alignment. The arithmetic and writing lessons should always be integrated with each other.

Words and verses for transcription *Work Book, pages 30–32*

The words on page 30 of the Work Book provide more practice in writing fluently and correctly. Make further speed tests and compare the results with those obtained previously.

The passages on pages 31 and 32 should be written very carefully and then systematically examined for the faults listed on page 27. They should be written a second time fairly slowly and carefully in an endeavour to avoid the errors made during the first attempt. Finally, the passages should be written a third time with reasonable speed and rhythm.

Even if the teacher has been obliged to spend extra time on certain sections of the work detailed in the scheme, there should still be time available before the end of the session for intensive revision.

Passages should continue to be given each week for transcription. From faults observed in writing these passages the teacher will find what revision and remedial instruction are most necessary. The children should be encouraged to develop the fluency and general excellence of their writing. Their practice in writing is not of itself sufficient. Unless the pupils are stimulated to take a pride in writing well and in writing fluently, progress will be unnecessarily slow. Marks should be awarded for speed of writing as well as for the general appearance and formation of letters.

Few sentences have been given in the Work Books for transcription, as this type of work will have received adequate attention during the informal writing periods throughout the year. During the remaining weeks of the session, simple sentences for transcription can profitably be included in the formal writing periods.

If I were an apple

If I were an apple
And grew upon a tree
I think I'd fall down
On a nice boy like me.

I wouldn't stay there
Giving nobody joy;
I'd fall down at once
And say "Eat me my boy."

Specimen page from Work Book One

THE SECOND YEAR: WORK BOOK TWO

Summary

Formal instruction—10 minutes daily

(1) Revision of basic writing techniques.

(2) Left-handed writers (see page 15).

(3) Assessment of level of achievement of individual pupils; remedial instruction.

(4) Revision of method of writing fluently all letters and numerals.

(5) Revision of method of writing together Group 1 and Group 2 letters.

(6) Practice in writing words containing Group 1 and Group 2 letters.

(7) Relative height of letters; parallelism of strokes; slope of writing.

(8) Writing together letters from Groups 1 and 3.

(9) Writing together letters from Groups 1 and 4.

(10) Cross ligatures; the letters *f*, *t* and *r*.

(11) Letters which do not join.

(12) Fluency of writing; assessment of speed and quality of writing.

Informal instruction

The work detailed in this scheme and illustrated in Work Book 2 is the work which is to be undertaken during the short, daily periods of formal teaching.

It is, however, essential that pupils have ample opportunity throughout the week for practising work covered during the formal lessons, and that the progress made during these lessons should be reflected in the writing produced in the service of other subjects.

All writing must be done as fluently as possible. Attention must be paid to correct posture, pencil-hold, and relaxation of muscles, every time the child writes.

General

The stages in which the formal work for the year may be attempted are shown below. Each page of the Work Book corresponds approximately to the amount of formal instruction which can be covered in one week. The rate of progress, however, will depend on the ability and previous training of the pupils, and the teacher should feel free to modify the scheme to meet the requirements of individual pupils and on occasion to take lessons out of sequence.

The work which is set out in the scheme for the first primary class is the foundation for all that follows in other classes. It is essential that this stage be mastered before new work is attempted, and for this reason the first few weeks of this scheme should be devoted to revision.

Scheme of Work

Revision of basic techniques and letter forms — *Work Book, pages 1–3*

Ensure that each child is provided with a seat and desk suited to his height so that it is possible for him to make unrestricted writing movements.

Observe each child while he is writing and look for faulty posture, failure to hold and use a pencil correctly, and failure to relax. Use the diagrams and explanations on page 1 of the Work Book to help the child to acquire satisfactory posture and pencil-hold. Give remedial instruction and assistance to individual children while the class is engaged in performing a pencil exercise. Help left-handed pupils in particular to acquire a satisfactory posture and pencil-hold. Stress the importance of relaxed muscles and give instruction in the type of exercises which pupils can perform for themselves at any time (see page 11 of the Teacher's Book).

Revise very briefly the method of writing all letters, capitals and numerals. Refer to the illustrations on page 3 of the Work Book. Letter forms should have progressed from the elementary prototype used at the beginning of the infant department to the form illustrated. Each letter and numeral should be written several times and each child should practise the letters which he writes unsatisfactorily.

Give the class practice in writing selected letters at speed without serious deterioration of the letter forms. Test the speed at which each child is able to write letters by asking the class to write a letter such as *a* or *b* as often as possible in one minute. Record the scores made by each child and check their progress by subsequent tests.

Revision of ligatures
between Group 1 and Group 2 letters — *Work Book, Pages 4–6*

Both teacher and pupil must constantly bear in mind that the exercise is *not* to join together two letters but to write together speedily and rhythmically the two letters in one continuous movement. Any join between two letters which does not facilitate such a movement is best left unlearned.

Give practice in writing Group 1 letters *a, c, d, e, h, i, k, l, m, n, t* and *u* quickly and well. Make sure that the incipient ligature rises at an angle of about 45° and makes an acute rounded turn like this;

l c d not lll codd

Unless the ligature rises at the correct angle the spacing between adjacent letters will not be correct.

Demonstrate on the blackboard how some of the simpler combinations such as *in*, *he* and *li* are to be written in one smooth, continuous movement and examine the examples illustrated on page 4 of the Work Book.

Give the children much practice in writing the combinations illustrated on page 4 of the Work Book. Each combination should be written at least a dozen times before the next combination is attempted. The work can be carried out in an exercise book or on any cheap type of paper.

Children should be encouraged to practise exercises from their work books at home or in free moments in class. If a soft black pencil is used the exercises can be written even on newspaper or over writing in an old exercise book. The more able pupils should be allowed to write pattern exercises and the less common combinations while the teacher helps pupils who are making slower progress. Give further instruction on the angle and slope made by a ligature, using exercises such as those shown on page 5 of the Work Book. There should be intensive practice in writing such combinations as *ne*, *an*, *en*, *un*, *ee*, *hi*, *le*, *de*, *te*, *tr*, *ly*, *cr*, *ev*, *ey*.

After further practice in writing pairs of letters, the children should write the words containing combinations of Groups 1 and 2 letters shown on page 6 of the Work Book: aim, any, air, cup, men, him, her, here, hum, hip, line, time, mine, lump, keen, key, mummy, miner. Each word should be written many times speedily and well before the next word is attempted.

Give practice in writing quickly and well words in which there are letters not joined, e.g. go, one, bay, ham, pin, wine, queen, view, let, hens, leg, limb, dirt, dumb, mend, is, you, pool, buzz, half, edge, vase, dog, down.

Relative size of letters *Work Book, page 7*

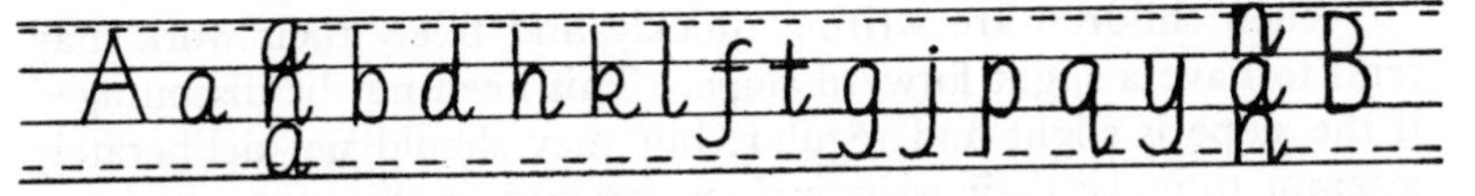

Let the pupils examine carefully the relative heights of the letters shown in the diagram on page 7 of the Work Book. Tall ascenders and capitals should be almost twice the height of the lower-case letters. Capitals are the same size as the ascenders. The letters *f* and *t* are not so tall as the other ascenders. The descenders are slightly less than twice the height of the lower-case letters, such as *o*, *a* and *n*.

The combinations of letters shown in the Work Book on page 7 can be written if desired, first of all between a double ruling, then on a single line on which the letters merely rest and finally on blank paper.

It is a great mistake to allow children to use ruled paper continually or even frequently. Ruled paper obviously enables a teacher to obtain reasonably tidy and regular writing with the minimum of effort on her part. Lines, however, prevent the child from learning how to make regular well-spaced writing and from learning to appreciate the relative heights of the letters. The sooner this crutch is dispensed with, the earlier will the child learn to write well.

Parallelism and slope of writing strokes *Work Book, page 8*

Explain what is meant by parallel lines. Illustrate on the blackboard the effect on writing produced by the lack of parallelism of up- and down-strokes and of ligatures:

Handwriting Handwriting

Give exercises in making rows of parallel strokes and in writing words, with special attention to the parallelism of up- and down-strokes and of ligatures.

When children are writing quickly and freely their work may tend to have a slight forward slope. This need not be discouraged if the slope is slight and regular; but they should not deliberately attempt to make their writing slope forward at this stage, and any child whose writing slopes excessively or irregularly should be made to revert to vertical writing.

A backward slope must not be permitted unless the writer is

left-handed. Such a slope will only occur if the pencil is held incorrectly, or if the body is twisted to the side.

How well can you write? *Work Book, page 9*

The children should write, carefully and fairly slowly, a passage such as is illustrated on page 9 of the Work Book. They should then examine minutely what has been written and check for the faults listed on the same page.

A routine should be established for the examination by children of their own writing. They should know what faults to look for and should be encouraged to criticise and correct their own writing exercises.

When the children under the guidance of the teacher have marked their writing errors, the passage should again be written carefully but not too slowly and an attempt made to avoid the previous faults. The passage can be written once more, this time at considerable speed.

Each effort should be examined as before for the faults listed on page 9.

Writing quickly and well *Work Book, page 10*

Give practice in writing sentences fairly slowly and carefully at first and then at speed. Note any deterioration of letter forms or ligatures, faulty spacing of letters, words and lines, and give remedial instruction and practice as required. Pay particular attention to crossing of *t*'s and *f*'s and dotting of *i*'s, to sprawling ligatures and to excessively tall or short ascenders and descenders.

A fairly satisfactory and commonly used test is to let the child write the sentence 'Mary had a little lamb' as often as he can in two minutes. The number of *letters* (not words) written in the two minutes is counted and divided by two to give the average number of letters written in one minute. This is the child's speed score. It will be satisfactory at this stage, and easier for the children to count their own scores, if the sentence is written for one minute only.

It will be found that in a normal class the writing speeds of children will vary very widely. It is common for the fastest writer to write at least three times as quickly as the slowest writer. For this reason it is difficult to fix writing speed norms for children of a given age. The speed at which a child writes will depend not only on his neuromuscular development but also on his writing techniques and style of letters, on the nature of his previous training in writing, on the amount of practice he has been given in writing speedily and rhythmically, and on the encouragement he has been given to take pride and pleasure in writing quickly and well.

The teacher should regularly test the writing speeds of the pupils and encourage them to test themselves occasionally at home as well as in school.

Writing together Group 1 and Group 3 letters *Work Book*, *pages 11–13*

The Group 1 letters, *a*, *c*, *d*, *e*, *h*, *i*, *k*, *l*, *m*, *n*, *t* and *u*, which end with incipient ligatures, can be made to join without pencil lift to the Group 3 letters, *b*, *f*, *h*, *k*, *l* and *t*. The difficulty in doing so is that the ligature must change direction halfway up if the space between the letters is to remain correct and if the type of fault illustrated below is to be avoided:

eh et if chilly

There should be an almost imperceptible lift of the pencil between the end of the incipient ligature and the starting point of the tall letter. At a later stage the better pupils may be able to join these pairs of letters without lifting the pencil from the paper. They should not, however, be encouraged to do so at this stage as no increase in speed or rhythm will be achieved, and the unnecessary and possibly badly made ligatures will merely detract from the legibility of the writing. The teacher's task at this stage is to ensure that pairs of letters from these groups are written well, with correct spacing and with considerable speed and rhythm.

Plenty of practice should be had in writing the pairs of letters illustrated in the Work Book on pages 11 and 12: *il*, *el*, *al*, *ll*, *if*, *th*, *et*, *ut*, *ct*, *nt*, *ht*, *tt*, *af*, *ef*, *lf*, *uf*, *ch*, *ul*, *ab*, *ak*, *ck*, *nk*, *cl*, *ub*, *tl*, *ek*, *eb*.

Give the children practice in writing at speed rows and pairs of letters such as those illustrated on page 12 of the Work Book. When they can write these speedily, rhythmically and with correct spacing, give them practice in writing words such as those illustrated on page 13.

Writing together Group 1 and Group 4 letters *Work Book, pages 14–16*

No attempt should be made at this stage to join letters with incipient ligatures to the Group 4 letters, *a*, *c*, *d*, *g*, *o* and *q*. Attempts to join without lifting the pencil will in many cases result in efforts such as this:

no no no instead of no

Exactly the same considerations and procedure apply to Groups 1 and 4 letters as did to Groups 1 and 3 letters. The teacher's task is to ensure that pupils learn to write combinations of these letters with correct spacing, speedily, rhythmically and well.

Children should be given plenty of practice in writing the combinations shown on Page 14 of the Work Book: *ic*, *no*, *ea*, *ca*, *co*, *lo*, *ha*, *ed*, *id*, *td*, *ng*, *eg*, *ig*, *ag*, *eq*. Practice in writing a few words containing these combinations can follow, e.g. iced, long, hall, hang.

Thereafter they should have practice in the pattern exercises and letter combinations shown on page 15 of the Work Book: *ma*, *na*, *ac*, *la*, *ld*, *ad*, *da*, *ha*, *to*, *ta*. In some pattern exercises, rows of letters are shown upside down or in a vertical column. Children are, of course, expected to turn their exercise books round so that the row of letters is written in the orthodox manner.

Practice in writing letter combinations should be followed by intensive practice in writing words containing these combinations. Words such as those shown on page 16 of the Work Book can be used, e.g. do, dog, not, into, lot, come, lid, end, lend, send, hand, bag, dig, hang, long, cage, lace, face, cake, coal, quick, each, lead, head, bead, teach, landed, added, account:

Writing quickly and well *Work Book, page 17*

Revise briefly the general instructions regarding posture, pencil-hold and relaxation.

The passage shown in the Work Book should be written very carefully but not too slowly.

Examine each child's work for badly made letters and ligatures; letters of incorrect size; incorrect spacing of letters, words and lines; and misalignment and general irregularity of writing. Deduct marks accordingly. Pupils should also examine their writing in the way explained on page 9 of the Work Book. Remedial instruction and practice should be given as required.

The passage should be written again very carefully but at a reasonable speed, care being taken to avoid the faults made in the first attempt.

The pupils should write the passage once more, but this time as speedily as they can without permitting the letters and ligatures to deteriorate too drastically. The result should be compared with the previous efforts.

Test the writing speed of each pupil in the way explained on page 10 of the Work Book.

Letters with cross-ligatures *Work Book, pages 18–20*

The letters *o*, *v* and *w* can be terminated with a short horizontal stroke which carries the pencil on to the beginning of most following letters.

Refer children to page 18 of the Work Book and demonstrate how the letters *o*, *v* and *w* can be joined to a following letter, e.g. *on*, *vi* and *wr*. The joining-stroke must be horizontal and at the same height as the top of the letter. It should not sag between one letter and the next and it must be of the right length so that the letters are correctly spaced. There must not be a loop at the top of an *o* before the beginning of the cross-stroke.

on vi wr not on vi wr

Give much practice in writing quickly and correctly the letters *o*, *v* and *w* with a ligature and then the more common combinations shown on page 18 of the Work Book: *on, om, ou, ov, ow, oy, or, oi, op, vi, wn, wr.*

When children can write these combinations speedily and well they should practise writing a few words which include them, e.g. win own, view, our, ton, lone, done, home, out, now, down, vinegar, noise, wrong, open, window, wide.

This should be followed by instruction on joining from *o*, *v* and *w* to the Group 4 letters *a*, *c*, *d*, *g*, and *o*. This join is not quite so easy as the preceding combinations.

Use the Work Book and a blackboard to show how a ligature of this type has to be taken over and round the top of the Group 4 letter to its starting point. Children should have intensive practice in writing pairs and then strings of *o*'s speedily and correctly. This can be followed by writing combinations such as *oa, oc, og, od, wa, wo, va, vo.* Words such as those shown on page 19 of the Work Book should be practised, e.g. look, low, hour, your, how, or, door, coal, cocoa, load, lock, wood, moon, noon, floor, poor, vine, violet, voice, van, valley, wall, water, would, woman, wrong.

No attempt should be made to ligature from *o*, *v* or *w* to the tall letters *f*, *t*, *b*, *h*, *k* and *l*, though there will be a strong inclination to do so once this joining stroke has been learned. Pupils should be given practice in writing words containing pairs of letters from Groups 4 and 3. The spaces between the letters in such words must be correct.

The words on page 20 of the Work Book should be given for practice: who, why, what, when, where, cool, pool, tool, fool, wool, cold, hole, cook, of, pot, job.

Pattern exercises such as those illustrated can be devised and practised by the children. The words illustrated on the lower half of page 20 will prove useful for intensive practice in writing this type of combination at speed.

No attempt should be made to ligature *o*, *v* or *w* to the letters *e*, *s* or *z*.

Joining from the letter f — *Work Book, page 21*

The cross-stroke of the letter *f* can be used to ligature to all small letters except *e* and *s*. It should not be used to ligature to tall letters. The cross-stroke should be straight, at the correct height and of a length which ensures that the two letters are correctly spaced.

Use the Work Book and blackboard to show how this cross-stroke is of help in writing a pair of letters speedily and as a rhythmical whole.

Practice in writing combinations such as *fi*, *fu*, *fr*, *fo* and *fa* should be followed by practice in writing words such as are illustrated on page 21 of the Work Book, e.g. fig, fill, fix, fin, fit, first, full, fun, furry, fume, fuel, fry, free, from, frog, frost, for, fog, four, fox, food, fan, fall, far, fast, faint.

Extra care should be taken in joining the cross-stroke to the beginning of oval letters. When two *f*'s occur together in a word, one cross-stroke may be used to cross the two letters. Similarly an *f* and *t* occurring together could be crossed by one stroke, but it is doubtful if there is any advantage in so doing.

The following words can be used for practice: off, cuff, stuff, puff, muff, fluff, toffee, left, gift, after, lift, soft.

Joining from the letter t

The cross-stroke of the letter *t* can be used in the same way as the stroke of the letter *f* to ligature to a following letter. It is used in this way by a number of writers, but such a ligature leads to difficulties not associated with the ligature derived from the bottom of the letter. As the pupils have already learned to make the latter form of ligature there seems little point in unlearning it and spending time in acquiring a new form. If, however, the teacher has a strong preference for using the cross-stroke as a ligature, and if continuity of instruction in later classes is assured, no great harm will result from learning this form.

Joining from the letter r *Work Book, pages 22 and 23*

The form of the letter *r* which has been taught so far is simple, distinctive, historically correct and aesthetically satisfying. It does not, however, ligature readily to a following letter, and when it is joined to *i*, *n*, *m*, *r*, *u* and *y* the resulting combination can be confusing:

n m rr ru ry

It is not altogether satisfactory to leave it unligatured to a following letter, as it is difficult to lift the pencil for the very short distance between the end of the *r* and the beginning of the next letter. A deliberate lift of this kind impairs the rhythm and speed of writing with the result that most adult writers devise for themselves some form of ligature to obviate the pencil-lift during speedy writing. Such ligatures are rarely satisfactory.

It is suggested that either the form which has already been taught can be used without ligatures to a following letter, or that a slightly modified form be adopted, such as is illustrated in the Work Book, and ligatured to the letters shown. It is most important that whatever form is adopted should continue to be taught and used in subsequent classes.

In the form illustrated on page 22 of the Work Book, the terminal stroke of the letter is a small loop instead of a slight downward curve. If this form is to be adopted, the teacher should use the methods described in the Infant Teacher's Book for teaching a new letter form to infants, e.g. tracing over the letter, tracing in the air and writing on the desk with the fingers. The children should then be given much practice in writing the new form on paper and in joining it to the letters *i*, *m*, *n*, *r*, *u* and *y*. Pattern exercises can be followed by practice in writing words containing these combinations, e.g. run, rip, turn, drum, rind, rich, ripe, rise, rub, rut, rule, rye, very, arm, firm, learn, merry, carry. These exercises can be followed by practice in joining *r* to the oval letters *a*, *c*, *d*, *g* and *o* as illustrated on page 23 of the Work Book.

Practice should then be given in pattern exercises and in writing words containing the combinations learned, e.g. ram, rag, rack, arch, march, larch, lard, word, board, rod, rope, rose, rock, argue, urge, rare, herd, large, roar, room, rain.

No attempt should be made to ligature *r* to the letter *s* or *z* or to tall letters. This form of *r* can be ligatured to an *e* by dropping the loop to the beginning of this letter. This ligature is used quite extensively, but it is not advocated.

Letters which never join *Work Book, page 24*

The Group 6 letters *b*, *g*, *j*, *p*, *q*, *s*, *x*, *y* and *z* *do not* join to a following letter. This should be known already, but revision at this stage will be helpful. Give practice in writing words containing these letters, e.g. best, busy, biggest, ghost, just, quiz, zebra, quest, press, sixty.

The letters *s* and *f* are of a very satisfying form with a distinctive curve at the top of the letters. On no account should a ligature be taken to the top. Both letters can deteriorate badly if carelessly made or if an attempt is made to join to them, and it should be impressed on children that the form of these letters must be preserved.

Practise words such as those on page 24 of the Work Book, e.g. first, left, fussy, jiffy, fifty, fuse, frost, soft, suffer, press.

Letters with incipient ligatures join easily to the letter *e* but no other letters do so, since *e* is unique in having its starting point near the bottom. In formal Italic Script the letter *e* is made with two strokes and this facilitates joins from *o*, *v*, *w*, *f*, *t*, and *r*. There is, however, no advantage to be gained from making an *e* in this way as letters with incipient ligatures do not easily join to it.

The words shown at the foot of page 24 of the Work Book illustrate the rules for writing *e* with another letter: lend, dine, cell, her, deer, rest, were, feel, seven, between, gentle, jelly, doe, pest, several.

All children should occasionally practise making patterns and borders from joined and unjoined letters. These patterns may be used to decorate handwork, book covers, Christmas cards or a page of formal writing. The more able children may at times be employed in making such patterns while the teacher is giving group or individual instruction to pupils who have not kept pace with the rest of the class.

Revision of all ligatures *Work Book, page 25*

All methods of ligaturing between letters have now been dealt with. These methods are summarised and illustrated on page 25 of the Work Book. The teacher and pupils should constantly bear in mind that joins between letters are undesirable unless they enable the letters to be written more speedily and rhythmically. Nevertheless, increase in speed of writing is no justification for joining letters if the resulting ligature detracts from the legibility and beauty of the writing.

The various methods of ligaturing letters should now be revised, and the children tested in writing them. Give remedial instruction to the class or individuals as required. While the less able pupils are practising ligatures they cannot make well, the more able children should be encouraged to write very speedily and well the words on page 25 and words from their spelling lists or class readers.

Revision of basic techniques and letter forms *Work Book, page 26*

Revise and give remedial instruction on good posture, relaxation of muscles, and the correct method of holding and using the pencil. The children should perform the exercises illustrated on page 2 of the Work Book to develop their skill in manipulating the pencil. These exercises should be performed at maximum speed on scraps of paper or even over writing in old exercise books. Children should be encouraged to do one of these pencil exercises before each attempt at formal writing.

All the letters of the alphabet should now be practised at maximum speed. Letter forms which deteriorate badly should receive attention. The exercise can be varied by having the children write very quickly a sentence containing all the letters of the alphabet, e.g. The quick brown fox jumps right over the lazy dog.

Let the children write the passage shown on page 26 carefully and well but not too slowly. All writing should now be performed rhythmically and at a reasonable speed.

Attention should be paid to formation and size of letters, parallelism of strokes, spacing of letters, words and lines, and to the placing of the writing on the page. The children should by now be accustomed to checking their writing exercises for the faults listed on page 9 of their Work Books.

This exercise can be followed by allowing the children to write on blank paper one or two verses from a poem known to them. They should be given some prior instruction as to the size of margins.

Revision of capitals *Work Book, page 27*

Revise the method of writing capital letters as illustrated on page 3 of the Work Book. Use some method such as the one illustrated on page 27 of the Work Book to stress the importance of making good legible capital letters.

Give practice in writing each capital letter very speedily and well. This can be followed by writing words starting with capitals, e.g. days of the week, months, seasons, countries, towns, counties and names of children in the class. Some of these are illustrated on page 27 of the Work Book. No attempt should be made to ligature from capitals.

Revision of numerals *Work Book, page 28*

Revise the method of writing all numerals as shown on pages 3 and 28 of the Work Book and give further practice. Refer to page 20 of this book for notes on the numerals advocated. Loops on 2, 4 and 7 should be prohibited, as such loops when badly made are the prime source of illegibility.

Practice should be given in writing numerals in straight rows and vertical columns on blank paper.

Show how to set out neatly and carefully the simple sums shown on page 28 and also the sums in current use in class.

Instruction and practice in the use of the symbols for money, weights and measures may well be given at this stage.

Layout of formal written work — *Work Book, pages 29 and 30*

Give elementary instruction in the layout of formal written work, e.g. letters, addresses on envelopes, invitations to parties, classroom notices, samples of handwriting for display, etc.

The appearance of written matter is enhanced by ample margins of the correct proportions. The bottom margin should be about twice the height of the top margin. On a single sheet, the side margins should be equal and may be the same size or slightly greater than the top margin.

Ask the children to study the layout of the material on page 29 of the Work Book, the letter on page 30 and the material on any of the pages of the Work Book.

Attention should be paid at all times to the layout of written work, but children should be given the opportunity at this stage of taking time to set out properly the examples of formal writing mentioned in the first paragraph.

Allow the children to write a letter similar to that on page 30 on blank paper. Attention should be paid to layout as well as to the quality of the writing.

Passages for transcription — *Work Book, pages 31 and 32*

For the remainder of the session the children can be given passages, such as those illustrated on pages 31 and 32 of the Work Book, to be written with great care and at a reasonable speed. The same or similar passages should also be written as fluently as possible without serious deterioration of the writing. During these remaining writing periods the teacher should pay constant attention to writing techniques and give assistance and remedial instruction to any child who produces faulty letter forms or ligatures.

The children should again be given speed tests and the results compared with those previously obtained.

The teacher should take every opportunity of stimulating the children's interest and pride in good writing. Progress is unlikely to be satisfactory unless the children believe that it is important to learn to write well and unless they constantly strive to increase the fluency and quality of their writing.

151, Abbey Street,
Eastown,
1st April, 1960

Dear John,

I am learning to write both quickly and well.

I must be able to write quickly so that my writing will help me with other lessons such as spelling, sums, writing letters and exercises.

It is also important to write clearly and well, so that others can read my writing easily.

Your friend,
Tom Brown

Specimen page from Work Book Two

THE THIRD YEAR: WORK BOOK THREE

Summary

Formal instruction—10 minutes daily

(1) Correction of faults of posture, pencil-hold and relaxation observed in individual pupils.

(2) Left-handed writers (see page 15).

(3) Revision of method of writing letters together and in writing words or parts of words as rhythmical wholes.

(4) Fluency—constant practice with pattern exercises, words and sentences to increase the speed and rhythm of writing ; regular use of the standard test of writing speed.

(5) Assessment of the quality of letter forms, regularity of slope and of the spacing of letters, words and lines.

(6) Introduction to the use of pen and ink using a smooth, rounded or a trench-pointed nib to produce *filiform* writing; scribbling and pattern exercises with pen and ink followed by the writing of letters, words and sentences with emphasis from the start on fluency.

Informal instruction

Opportunities must be sought during the writing of class work to incorporate the lessons learned during the periods of formal instruction, but the emphasis should be placed on the writing of meaningful material fluently and legibly rather than on the excellence of letter forms.

Neat and tidy work must always be demanded.

General

It is essential that the teacher be familiar with the content of the schemes for the earlier stages and that pupils be given instruction appropriate to their level of achievement.

From this stage onwards, the writing illustrated in this book and in Work Books 3 and 4 has a slight forward slope. Children who write fluently may already have begun to slope their writing in this way, especially if their writing paper is tilted to the left as shown in the illustration on page 10. They should be encouraged to write with the slight degree of forward slope illustrated in the Work Books; but children who produce fluent, vertical writing should not be forced to change their style.

Scheme of Work

Revision of basic techniques and letter forms *Work Book, pages 1–3*

Ensure that each child is provided with a seat and desk suited to his height.

Assess the level of achievement of each child in the class in respect of (1) writing techniques, (2) quality and fluency of writing. Determine what remedial instruction is required and group the children accordingly.

With the help of the diagram on page 1 of the Work Book revise the method of sitting at a desk which best enables a child to make free writing movements. Give remedial instruction as required and pay constant attention throughout the year to correct posture.

A pencil is held in exactly the same manner as a pen at a later stage. Use the diagrams on pages 1 and 19 of the Work Book to show how the pencil should be held. It *must* be held lightly.

Much practice in scribbling and pattern-making at speed is necessary to develop the correct hold and use of a pencil. The pattern exercises illustrated on page 2 may be used for this purpose. While the less able children are receiving individual help and instruction from the teacher in the basic techniques, the more able pupils could perform the pattern exercises shown on these pages.

Stress the importance of relaxed muscles when writing and revise the relaxation exercises which the children can perform themselves.

The small letters, capitals and numerals to be written with pencil (and later with pen) are illustrated on page 3 of the Work Book. Revise briefly the method of writing each character and give practice in writing them well with speed and rhythm. Further practice should be devoted to characters which the pupil is unable to write with satisfactory quality and fluency.

Revision of ligatures *Work Book, page 4*

Revise the general principles involved in the ligaturing of letters with particular reference to Group 1 and Group 2 letters.

Use examples such as those illustrated on page 4 of the Work Book to give children practice in writing pairs of letters and words containing such combinations. See Work Books 1 and 2 for further examples and detailed procedure.

Work Book, page 5

Revise further the method of writing together pairs of letters, placing particular emphasis on the correct formation of ligatures. The curve at the base of the ligature should be a sharp smooth curve.

Joining to tall letters *Work Book, page 6*

No attempt should be made to carry ligatures to the starting points of the Group 3 letters *b*, *f*, *h*, *k*, *l*, and *t*.

With the help of the illustrations on page 6 of the Work Book, revise the method of writing a Group 1 letter followed by a Group 3 letter. The pencil should be carried quickly but smoothly and rhythmically from the end of the up-stroke to the starting point of the tall letter. The pencil should skim, without marking, the surface of the paper.

If letters are correctly spaced the upstroke will meet the tall letter midway and the two letters will appear to be joined.

Joining to oval letters *Work Book, pages 7 and 8*

Revise the method of carrying the pencil to the beginning of the Group 4 letters *a*, *c*, *d*, *g*, *o* and *q*. Give practice in writing quickly and correctly pairs of letters such as those illustrated on page 7 of the Work Book.

This can be followed by practice involving the patterns on page 8 and then the writing of the pairs of letters and words illustrated. Emphasis should be placed on writing with speed and rhythm as well as on the correct formation and spacing of letters.

Cross-stroke ligatures *Work Book, page 9*

Revise the method of using the cross-strokes from the letters *o*, *v* and *w* as ligatures:

win our town moving

The cross-stroke must be short so that the spacing between letters is correct, but at this stage it need not be perfectly straight. A very slight dip will help to increase the speed and rhythm of writing. When the simple cross-stroke can be written quickly and correctly, instruction should be given in carrying these types of ligatures to the beginning of oval letters.

Cross-strokes from *o*, *v* and *w* should not join to the tops of tall letters nor to the letters *e*, *s* and *z*.

Joining from the letters f and r *Work Book, page 10*

Revise the method of using the cross-stroke of the letter *f* as a ligature to all small letters except *e* and *s*. It should not be ligatured to tall letters. Give plenty of practice in making this join quickly and well.

The letter *r* may still present difficulty to some children and time may have to be spent in revising the method of writing this letter when it is joined to a following letter.

Pairs of letters and appropriate words to be used for the revision of joins from *f* and *r* are illustrated on page 10 of the Work Book.

Letters which do not join *Work Book, page 11*

The Group 6 letters *b*, *g*, *j*, *p*, *q*, *s*, *x*, *y* and *z* do not join easily or naturally to a following letter. No attempt should be made to do so by means of a ligature which must inevitably detract from the legibility of the writing and which is unlikely to improve the speed and rhythm of performance. Children should be given exercises in writing unjoined letters such as those illustrated on page 11 of the Work Book. The aim should be to improve the quality of the letters, to achieve correct spacing and to increase the fluency of writing words containing unjoined letters.

Practice in ligaturing — *Work Book, page 12*

The method of writing together all groups of letters has now been revised. Pupils should be given intensive practice in writing with considerable speed and rhythm words suggested by the teacher or selected by themselves from their class readers. At no time should they be allowed to write at such a speed that gross deterioration of letter forms takes place; but there must be a continual striving to increase the fluency and improve the quality of the writing.

Particular attention should be paid at this stage to the correct spacing of letters in words. The words on page 12 of the Work Book should be practised until the children are reasonably competent at spacing letters correctly. The passage illustrated on page 12 should also be written carefully but not too slowly and then examined for errors in spacing. It should then be written a second time more quickly and again examined for errors.

Size and parallelism of letters — *Work Book, page 13*

With the help of the illustration on page 13 of the Work Book, revise the rules regarding the relative size of letters. Blank paper should be used for practice in writing letters of the correct size.

A a e i o u b d h k l f t g j p q y z Z

Use the illustrations on page 13 to emphasise how neat and tidy writing depends a great deal on parallel down-strokes and up-strokes.

The children should practise writing the words illustrated and then check their work for parallelism of strokes.

Spacing of letters, words and lines *Work Book, page 14*

Revise briefly the rules for the spacing of letters, words and lines, and practise the words and sentences illustrated.

Faults to look for *Work Book, page 15*

Children are unlikely to make satisfactory progress unless they know what is wrong with their writing and strive to eradicate their faults. It is helpful if they can adopt a routine for assessing the quality of their writing and they should be encouraged to apply frequently some such check as is shown on page 15 of the Work Book.

Writing at speed *Work Book, pages 16 and 17*

The speed as well as the quality of writing must receive constant attention and assessment. Exercises such as those illustrated on pages 2 and 16 of the Work Book should be used very frequently to give the child practice in using his pencil correctly and with considerable fluency. Children should be encouraged to compete with each other in writing at speed. They should be given timed tests and their writing speed determined regularly by the standard method outlined on page 16 of the Work Book. (See the Scheme of Work for the second year, page 57).

A passage for writing in a given time is illustrated on page 17 of the Work Book. Many children at this stage should be able to write at least 100 letters per minute.

How well can you write? *Work Book, page 18*

Passages from the class reader can occasionally be given for writing practice, but the child must be consciously attempting to improve the quality and speed of his writing when performing an exercise of this type. Mere practice in writing is not enough. Such passages should be fairly short and should be written two or three times.

The first attempt may be written with great care but not so slowly that the rhythm of writing is sacrificed. Subsequent attempts should be written with increased speed and rhythm. The child should apply the routine check on the quality of his writing after each attempt.

Writing with pen and ink *Work Book, pages 19 and 20*

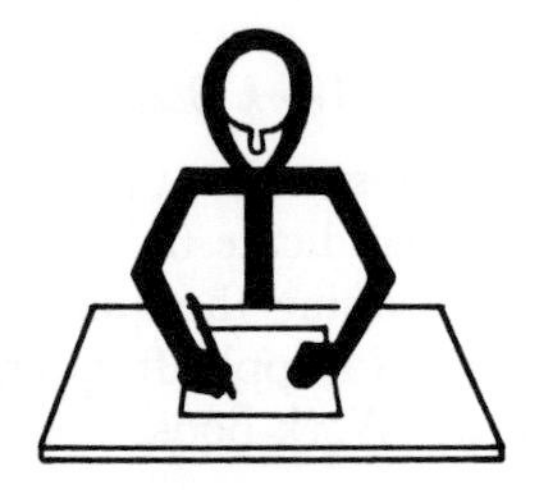

Children who have learned to hold and use a pencil in the correct manner and who have acquired satisfactory habits of posture and relaxation, will have little or no difficulty in learning to use pen and ink. If a fountain pen with a smooth, rounded point or a dip pen with a similar type of nib is used, the very minimum of help from the teacher will be required. On no account should a finely pointed, flexible pen be used.

In this scheme, a pen with a rounded point, which produces unshaded writing, is used as a means of introducing children to writing with ink. The change to the use of a square-edged pen, which produces a much more satisfying and attractive style of writing, is dealt with in Work Book 4, but can be attempted at an earlier stage if desired.

If a dip pen is used, the holder must not be narrow and good quality ink should be used. The teacher should show the child how to dip the pen to the required depth in the ink, how to remove surplus ink from the nib before writing, and how to wipe the nib clean after use.

The following points must receive attention:

(1) the pen *must* be held very lightly

(2) it should press very lightly on the paper

(3) it should be held in the same way as a pencil. (See diagrams on pages 1 and 19 of the Work Book.)

The pen should make an angle of not more than 45° with the paper, and the end should point along the line of the forearm to a point outside the right shoulder. It should not be turned or twisted by the fingers and the angle it makes with the paper should remain constant. If the children are to write from the outset with complete ease, freedom and pleasure, these requirements should only be mentioned briefly at the outset but should receive detailed instruction and attention later on when scribbling and shading exercises, such as those on pages 19 and 20 of the Work Book, are being done. Children should not be asked to write letters or words with care and exactitude until they have acquired confidence and skill in using a pen. Much practice should first be given to undirected scribbling and shading exercises. These may be followed by directed movements such as those on page 20, and it is during the performance of these exercises that the teacher should give any necessary detailed instructions in the correct method of using the pen.

When children have gained confidence in using a pen and can perform shading exercises with a considerable degree of speed and rhythm, they should progress to the writing of running-strokes and joining-strokes. These must be performed speedily and rhythmically from the start, and only when each child has acquired the ability to do this should letters and words be attempted.

The letters i, l, t, n, and u *Work Book, page 21*

The first letters to be written in ink should be *i*, *l*, *t*, *n* and *u* which consist mainly of a simple vertical stroke and ligature. When these letters can be written correctly with considerable ease and speed, words containing them, such as those on page 21 of the Work Book, should be practised.

The letters m, h and k; the letter e *Work Book, page 22*

Rhythmical pen exercises are followed by writing the letters *m*, *h* and *k*. These letters, and words containing them, should be written with as great ease, speed, rhythm and quality as the child attains when using a pencil.

Much time may need to be spent in writing the letter *e* quickly and correctly. Care should be taken to ensure that the loop of this letter is not filled in. Suitable words for practice are illustrated on page 22 of the Work Book.

The oval letters *Work Book, page 23*

Practice in writing the oval letters *a*, *c*, *d*, *g*, *o*, *q*, *b* and *p* should be preceded and accompanied by the writing of continuous ellipses and spirals, with clockwise and anti-clockwise movements as appropriate.

When these letters can be written correctly with the desired degree of speed and rhythm, the words on page 23 of the Work Book should be practised.

The other letters *Work Book, page 24*

The remaining letters of the alphabet as well as suitable words for practice are shown on page 24 of the Work Book.

Ligatures *Work Book, pages 25 and 26*

The children should now know the rules for ligaturing letters and should have written a number of words in ink. The exercises on pages 25 and 26 of the Work Book revise these rules and give suitable words for practice. The teacher's task is to ensure that such words are written fluently, speedily and well, and that the children strive to write with a steady, flowing movement across the page.

Capitals and numerals *Work Book, page 27*

Little difficulty should be experienced in writing capitals and numerals in ink.

The letters, numerals and practice material are illustrated on page 27 of the Work Book.

Intensive practice in writing capital letters is provided by writing words or sentences using only capital letters.

Neat and tidy writing *Work Book, page 28*

Neat and attractive writing is characterised by regularity. The teacher should amplify the instructions and illustrations given on page 28.

(1) The same letters should always be exactly of the same size and of the same shape.

(2) The bottoms of the small letters must all lie on the same line. The tops must also all be in a straight line.

(3) Letters of the same type must always be of the same height.

(4) Down-strokes and up-strokes should be parallel.

(5) The space between letters in a word, whether the letters are joined or unjoined, should be correct. This does not mean that there is always exactly the same distance between any pair of letters.

(6) There is almost always the same space between words in a sentence. At this stage the space is approximately the width of the letter *a* together with its joining-stroke.

(7) Lines of writing should run straight across the page.

(8) The space between successive lines of writing should always be the same and it should allow the tops of tall ascenders to keep clear of the tails of descenders in the line above.

No teacher should expect or even desire children to become so proficient in keeping these rules that their writing attains the mechanical perfection of the printed page. Nor should children be so burdened with rules of this kind that spontaneity and pleasure are drained from their writing. They should know, however, the goal at which they are aiming and they should be able to recognise and attempt to correct faults which occur.

Writing carefully and well — *Work Book, pages 29 and 30*

The words and the verse on page 29 of the Work Book and the passage on page 30 should be written with considerable care and then examined for the faults listed in the previous section. They should then be written a second time as speedily and fluently as possible but without any deterioration of ligatures or letter forms. Any remaining weaknesses should be improved by further practice, and if time permits the teacher may select other short but interesting passages of prose and poetry.

It would be appropriate at this stage to test the children's speed in writing with a pen. The standard test should be used and the results compared with those previously obtained when using a pencil.

Writing a letter — *Work Book, page 31*

By this stage children will have had some practice in writing a letter. Page 31 of the Work Book shows one of the ways in which a letter may be set out. The teacher may use this as a starting point for lessons on the importance of setting out work well on a page, using the correct margins and blank spaces. The setting out of the material on other pages of the Work Book can be used to illustrate the points made.

Children should have plenty of practice in laying out their work by writing letters, addressing envelopes, writing invitation cards and replies, notices, posters, and, of course, by the tidy and attractive arrangement of arithmetical and all other written school work.

Writing a verse — *Work Book, page 32*

Page 32 of the Work Book shows another way of setting out a verse. Comment on the proportion of written work to blank space and draw attention to the starting points of the short and long lines. Compare this layout with the arrangement of the verse on page 29.

The children should be given the opportunity of writing this and other poems, paying considerable attention to good letter forms, but writing as fluently as possible.

The arrangement of the material on the page in an attractive and pleasing manner should always be expected.

Additional work

If time permits after the work detailed in the scheme has been covered, the teacher should revise and consolidate the work covered during the session.

Assessments should be made of the quality and fluency of the writing of each child in the class. While remedial instruction is given to the less able, the better writers can be set exercises to develop the quality and fluency of their writing. Aimless practice by the better pupils must be avoided. They must be set specific tasks with the aim of consciously improving some aspect of their writing and a constant check must be made on the standard of their work.

All children should have exercises in making patterns which can be used to decorate notices, posters, and pages of formal writing. Short passages can be given for transcription with some definite aim in view such as improving the quality of letters, capitals, numerals and ligatures, improving the regularity of slope and spacing, and increasing the fluency of the writing. Children should acquire the habit of applying routine checks on the quality and speed of their writing.

The teacher should make speed checks at regular intervals and encourage children to compete with each other in the production of beautiful and fluent writing.

45, Castle Road
Bridgetown
4th. January 1961

Dear Mary,

Since my last letter to you I have been learning to write with pen and ink.

When you are writing in ink you must be very sure that you are holding your pen correctly. If you do that you will find it just as easy to write quickly and well with a pen as with a pencil.

Your sincere friend,

Jane Smith

Specimen page from Work Book Three

THE FOURTH YEAR: WORK BOOK FOUR

Introduction

Handwriting is a very complex motor-skill which develops slowly as a result of maturation and practice. By the time children are starting Work Book 4 the majority will have acquired a degree of muscular co-ordination sufficient to enable them to write a fairly free and mature hand with speed and rhythm. The main task of the teacher at this stage is, therefore, to foster this development by helping the child to write with greater uniformity and by ensuring that he strives to write in wholes rather than by a succession of separate strokes, so that his writing becomes more and more a rhythmical succession of movements.

The scheme for this stage indicates how the teacher may help the child to develop these attributes of a skilled writer, but it is not possible to illustrate this aspect of the work to any great extent in the Work Book. Part of Work Book 4 consists of a very necessary revision of earlier work, and the child is expected to perform these revision exercises with ever increasing fluency and skill. But they must be regarded not only as a revision of previous work, but also as practice material for developing skill in writing both a formal set hand and an extremely fluent and legible hand for everyday use.

Some children will in time be able to write a formal hand of a quality equalling or even excelling that illustrated in the Work Book. When the same children write with considerable ease and speed it is inevitable that the appearance of their writing will change. Writing performed at speed is unlikely to possess the excellence of letter forms which characterises a formal hand, but it can equal or even excel a formal hand in legibility, character and in the aesthetic quality and linear beauty that comes from freedom and fluency of production.

It is wrong to assume that this kind of writing is inferior. It is the teacher's prime task to encourage the development of just such a hand—a legible, fast-flowing, rhythmic and individual style of writing which will meet the needs of a child in school and in adult life.

Children must, however, continue to pay constant attention to the production of excellent letter forms and to develop a high standard of formal writing such as is illustrated in the Work Book.

Summary

Formal instruction—10 minutes daily

(1) Brief revision of basic writing techniques.

(2) Left-handed writers (see page 15).

(3) Filiform writing with pen and ink; further practice in writing letters, words and parts of words as rhythmical wholes.

(4) Fluency—constant practice with pattern exercises, words and sentences to increase the speed and rhythm of writing; regular assessment of the speed of writing.

(5) Practice in improving the quality of letters and the regularity of slope and spacing of letters, words and lines; assessment of the quality of the writing.

(6) Instruction in the use of a square-edged pen to produce shaded writing; practice in writing letters, words and sentences until a square-edged pen can be used with ease and confidence.

(7) Practice in writing a formal, set hand and also a free, cursive hand; assessment of speed and quality of both formal and free hands.

Informal instruction

The work detailed in this scheme and illustrated in Work Book 4 is the work which is to be undertaken during the short, daily periods of formal teaching.

It is, however, essential that pupils have ample opportunity throughout the week for practising work covered during the formal lessons and that the progress made during these lessons should be reflected in the writing produced in the service of other subjects.

Children must have plenty of practice in writing speedy, cursive writing so that when they enter a secondary school they are equipped with a fast, mature and extremely legible hand.

General

Children in a class will vary widely in ability and achievement. Instruction must be suited to the needs of each child and the teacher must, therefore, be familiar with the content of the schemes for earlier stages.

Scheme of Work

Revision of basic techniques *Work Book, pages 1–3*

Make sure that each child is provided with a seat and desk suited to his height.

Explain with the aid of the diagrams on page 1 of the Work Book why it is necessary to sit in this way. Ensure that children always assume a good writing posture.

With the help of the diagrams on page 1, revise the correct method of holding a pencil or a pen. Explain why the hand must only touch the paper lightly. (See page 9)

Stress the importance of relaxation exercises. (See page 12)

The exercises on page 2 of the Work Book should first be written in pencil and then with a smooth-pointed pen. Each exercise should be written several times, latterly with very considerable speed and rhythm. This will help children to hold and use a pencil and a pen in the desired manner. While the children are writing the exercises, the teacher will have an opportunity of assessing individuals and of giving remedial instruction in the basic writing techniques.

Use the exercises on page 3 for the same purpose. Each exercise should be performed several times with both pencil and pen, at first moderately slowly but with increased speed each time. Each exercise must be performed smoothly, steadily and rhythmically or the main value of the exercise will be lost. Do not progress to the next page until the children have learned to move their pencils and pens with a steady rhythmical, up-and-down movement at all writing speeds. Even the groups of unjoined letters must be written at a steady speed.

Revision of letters — *Work Book, page 4*

Some letters, and words containing these letters, are illustrated on page 4 of the Work Book. These are to be written with pencil and with pen. Most children should have learned in the previous class to write these well. The emphasis at this stage must be not merely to write these letters and words well, but to write them with a smooth steady rhythmical movement whether they are written moderately slowly or at very great speed.

The teacher should now be in a position to assess the level of achievement of each child in the class and to group children accordingly for instruction suited to their needs.

The letters a, c, d, g, o and q — *Work Book, page 5*

Ask the children to write the sentence shown at the top of page 5 of the Work Book. It should be written once fairly slowly and carefully and then a second time with more speed and freedom. The children should examine the oval letters *a*, *c*, *d*, *g*, *o* and *q* in both attempts and compare the quality of their letters with those on page 5 of the Work Book.

Remedial instruction and further practice in writing these letters smoothly and well at speed should proceed as follows:

(1) Practise the rhythmical elliptical anti-clockwise movement required to write the bodies of these letters.

(2) When the ovals can be made well with a smooth, steady movement, the complete letters should be practised in the same manner.

(3) Words containing these letters should then be practised until they can be written speedily, rhythmically and well.

The average child should now be able to write each letter at a speed of 70 to 100 letters per minute.

The letters p and b — *Work Book, page 6*

Revision and practice in writing the letters *p* and *b* should follow the procedure detailed in the previous section, the emphasis being on rhythm and speed as well as quality.

The letters s, e and r — *Work Book, page 7*

Revise and give further practice in writing the letters *s*, *e* amd *r* in the manner illustrated in the Work Book. Practice should continue until each letter can be written speedily and well, even with the eyes closed.

f, j, k and y, and letters with tails — *Work Book, page 8*

The letters *f*, *j*, *k* and *y* should now be revised and practice concentrated on those which are written least well.

This should be followed by practice in writing words which contain these letters.

The length and shape of the tails of letters which go below the line may be revised at this stage.

Size and slope of letters — *Work Book, page 9*

Revise the instructions regarding the relative size of letters and the parallelism of strokes. Children should write speedily and rhythmically words such as those illustrated on page 9 of the Work Book.

Further practice should be devoted to writing at speed, words containing letters which are consistently written incorrectly.

If posture and pen-hold are correct, the parallelism and slope of strokes will cause little serious difficulty when the children are writing at speed.

Writing-paper turned in an anti-clockwise direction, as shown in the diagram on page 9 of the Work Book, helps to improve regularity of slope. The paper should be turned so that its major axis lies in the same direction as the line of the forearm. Down-strokes tend to be made towards the centre of the body.

Left-handed children will be helped if the paper is rotated in a clockwise direction. The child in this case may tend to slope his writing backwards, but if by placing the paper in this way his task is eased, no objection should be taken to the backward slope.

Revision of ligatures *Work Book, page 10*

Revise the method of writing together Group 1 and Group 2 letters. Emphasise that it is not a case of joining one letter to another but of writing together two or more letters in one continuous rhythmical movement. The pairs of letters and words illustrated on page 10 of the Work Book should be practised until they can be written very quickly and well in this way. It must not be assumed that because it is possible to write a word such as 'minimum' without stopping or lifting the pencil at any point, it is necessary or even desirable to do so. Children at this stage are unlikely to be able to write solely by movement of the forearm with only the tips of the fourth and fifth fingers touching the paper. As long as they write with the wrist or ball of the hand resting lightly on the paper and mainly by movement of the wrist, hand and fingers, the hand will have to move across the page in a series of interrupted movements and a break in the middle of a long word will be necessary. As muscular control develops, they will become increasingly able to write more than four or five letters as a connected whole, but it is doubtful if at any stage there is any advantage to be gained by trying to do so.

Cross-stroke ligatures *Work Book, page 11*

Ask the children to write the sentence illustrated and then to examine the joins they have made from the letters *o*, *v* and *w*. Give what remedial instruction is necessary on the method of making joins from these letters.

The emphasis in this lesson must be on making the cross-stroke correctly, on the correct spacing of the letters and on avoiding jerky movements when writing the letters together.

Give practice in writing the letters and words illustrated, paying particular attention to these points.

Revise joins from the letters *f* and *r* in the same way. Much time may have to be spent on the letter *r* as it is difficult to write this letter correctly and at the same time maintain a steady rhythmical writing movement:

frfrfrfrfr ririririr rororororo

Joining to tall or oval letters *Work Book, page 12*

At this stage, all the methods of ligaturing letters may be revised and progress assessed. While some children are receiving remedial instruction in writing letters together, the more able should practise hard to increase the speed, rhythm and excellence with which they write words containing joined letters.

Explain why the pencil is lifted between the up-strokes of Group 1 letters and Group 3 (tall) or Group 4 (oval) letters.

(a) Ugly joins detract from the legibility of the writing:

al ab ao ac

(b) Ugly joins result in the incorrect spacing of letters :

although

(c) Ugly joins result in the loss of speed and rhythm.

It is quite wrong to assume that by joining every letter in a word the speed and rhythm of writing is increased. A few simple experiments which children can try for themselves make this apparent. Write quickly and rhythmically for one minute each :

(a) rows of the letter *a* without joins between the letters.

(b) rows of the letter *a* with each letter joined to the next.

Count the number of letters written in each case to find if one method is appreciably faster than the other.

Which of the two ways, if either, did the children find to be the easier and more rhythmical?

Repeat the experiment, writing the words *account*, *slightly*, *nineteen*, *thrill* with

(a) no letters joined

(b) all letters joined

(c) joins between letters as recommended in this scheme

Letters which do not join *Work Book, page 13*

Ask the children to write the sentence illustrated at the top of page 13 of the Work Book and then to examine what they have written. They should not have attempted to make joins from the letters *b*, *g*, *j*, *p*, *q*, *s*, *x*, *y* or *z* to a following letter. There is no advantage to be gained by making such joins.

The spacing between unjoined letters must be correct and the rhythm of writing must be maintained whether or not letters are joined. The children should write the letters and words illustrated, keeping these requirements in mind.

Capital letters and numerals may be revised briefly at this stage. Practise writing sentences using capital letters only.

Writing smoothly and steadily *Work Book, page 14*

The child should by now realise the importance of being able to write with smooth, steady and rhythmical movements. The continuous ovals, lines, joined and unjoined letters and words on page 14 of the Work Book should all be practised with this requirement in mind. The child must learn to write rows of joined and unjoined letters, words and sentences across the full width of the page with a smooth, steady movement of the pen.

Such practice may at first be carried out at a moderately slow speed, but the aim must be to develop speed without losing rhythm.

How well can you write? *Work Book, page 15*

A child is unlikely to improve unless he knows what constitutes good writing. He should be able to recognise defects in his own writing, assess its quality and thus know if improvement is being made.

Page 15 of the Work Book lists points which are characteristic of good writing. It is a good idea for the child to learn by rote a summary such as this and use it frequently to assess the quality of his writing and to recognise progress as it occurs.

A short passage such as that illustrated should be written fairly slowly and carefully and a detailed check applied. Practice should then be aimed at removing the particular faults discovered.

The passage should be written a second time at moderate speed and a third time rhythmically, but at fairly considerable speed, and the same procedure as above followed.

Writing quickly *Work Book, page 16*

The children will already be well aware that writing which is performed very slowly and with great care differs in several respects from that produced freely and at considerable speed.

Explain the characteristics of the formal set hand and of the fast cursive hand. Both must be written smoothly and rhythmically and have a high degree of regularity and legibility. Children must never be permitted to write carelessly or at such a speed that legibility is impaired.

From now on there must be concurrent development of a formal hand and of a free, speedy hand for everyday use.

The speed of writing for the free hand should be measured frequently by the method outlined on page 16 of the Work Book.

Excellence of letter forms and regularity and rhythm of production rather than speed are the desirable qualities of the formal hand.

Writing freely and easily *Work Book, page 17*

Writing can only reach a high degree of rhythmic excellence when the writer becomes so proficient that he no longer has to pay conscious attention to the mechanics of writing or to the production of correct letter forms; but during the formal lessons detailed in this scheme it is precisely these aspects of the skill to which he must pay conscious attention.

Through constant practice and attention during the formal writing periods, the basic writing techniques and the rules for the production of good writing must be acquired as habits. These habits will then take control when the subject matter of what is being written, rather than the writing itself, is of prime importance.

Constant attention must be paid by the teacher to the basic writing techniques and to the manner in which the pupils write. It is often much more important to pay attention to the writer than to what is written.

Verse for transcription *Work Book, page 18*

A poem in formal writing is illustrated in the Work Book. Children should write this poem slowly and carefully and assess their efforts in the manner described in the section dealing with page 15. After practice has been devoted to curing any faults discovered, the passage may be written again, carefully and rhythmically, but with a little more speed. The passage may be written a third time fairly quickly, bearing in mind the considerations previously mentioned when writing a formal hand.

Most of the common forms of punctuation marks are used in the poem illustrated on page 18 of the Work Book. It may therefore be convenient at this stage to explain how punctuation marks should be made and to give practice in writing them correctly.

Shaded writing *Work Book, page 19*

From this point onwards Work Book 4 deals with the writing of good letters using a square-edged pen and with the steps taken to acquire a formal and a cursive hand in shaded writing. The development of a free cursive hand must not be neglected in favour of a very formal hand.

The exercises will, at first, have to be written slowly and carefully with the square-edged pen, but there must also be ample opportunity for writing them as fluently as possible with both pencil and pen.

Most of the written exercises in other subjects will continue to be in pencil, but there must be opportunities of putting into practice lessons learned during the periods of formal instruction. When the child has become proficient in the use of the square-edged pen, he may use it for some routine purposes such as taking notes, and for informal class exercises. Only towards the end of the primary stage should the most proficient writers be encouraged to use a fountain pen with a square nib for most of their written work. The teacher must be careful, however, to ensure that the teaching of a subject does not suffer from the premature use of pen and ink, and that children are not inhibited from expressing their thoughts in writing because of lack of skill in the use of a new writing instrument. Page 19 of the Work Book illustrates the difference, and the reason for this difference, between writing produced with a round nib and that produced with a square nib. The teacher can amplify and illustrate these differences by using lettering chalk on the blackboard.

It should be emphasised that (a) the square-edge must always lie flat on the surface of the paper ; (b) the pen must always point in the same direction; (c) there is no change of pressure on the pen for up- and down-strokes.

Children should first try to make thick and thin strokes. They will find that the edge of the nib sticks on the paper and that the pen scratches unless the edge is kept quite flat on the paper. A broad nib should be issued in the early stages of instruction so that the edge can be seen on the paper and so that the drag of the pen can be felt when a thick down-stroke is made. A fountain pen with interchangeable point units or a dip pen with a reservoir nib is preferable to an ordinary dip pen.

Practice in shaded writing *Work Book, page 20*

Initial instruction in the use of a square-edged pen is continued on this page of the Work Book and rules for its use are tabulated.

The children should have practice in the use of the pen by writing words, sentences and the exercises illustrated. Only when they have gained confidence and can make the elementary strokes reasonably well should they proceed to the next lesson.

Thin, thick and medium strokes *Work Book, page 21*

Pupils should now be ready to learn to write the main strokes, not merely correctly, but with a considerable degree of ease and fluency. Practice should continue until they can do so.

A medium width of nib can be used at this and at all future stages. When the running stroke can be written fluently and correctly with an incipient ligature, the letters *i*, *l* and *t* and the words illustrated should be practised until they can be written with complete ease and confidence.

The letters n, m, h and u *Work Book, page 22*

The exercises, the letters *n*, *m*, *h* and *u* and the words containing them on page 22 of the Work Book should now be practised until a considerable degree of skill and fluency is acquired. This very formal and perhaps uninteresting practice should be leavened by allowing the children to use their square pens to make rhythmic patterns and to write some of their class exercises. In this and in the next few lessons the teacher should endeavour to maintain interest in the development of handwriting skill even though there may not be much of inherent interest in the formal exercises which are illustrated.

The letters o, c, a, d, g and q *Work Book, page 23*

Practise writing the oval letters *o*, *c*, *a*, *d*, *g* and *q*, and the words illustrated on page 23 of the Work Book.

Draw attention to (a) the variation in thickness of the line in the oval part of the letters. This will be correct only if the pen is held and used in the proper manner; (b) the sloping axis of the oval; (c) the angle between the oval and the beginning of the tail of the letter.

The letters p, b and e *Work Book, page 24*

Practise writing the letters *p*, *b* and *e*, and the words which contain these letters. Emphasis must be placed not merely on good letter forms but also on the ability to write them speedily and rhythmically.

The letters f, r, k and s *Work Book, page 25*

Practise writing the letters *f*, *r*, *k* and *s* and the words illustrated, in the same way as before.

The other letters *Work Book, page 26*

Practise writing in the same way as before the letters *j*, *y*, *v*, *w*, *x* and *z*, and the words illustrated.

Revise all the lower case letters and allow individual pupils to practise the letters they write least well.

Revision of ligatures *Work Book, page 27*

Revise quickly the methods of writing letters together and give ample practice in writing words which contain ligatured letters.

Remind children (a) that up-stroke joins are not made to the tops of tall letters or to oval letters; (b) that the spacing of letters in a word must be correct; (c) that a word must be written with a smooth, steady, continuous movement.

Suitable words for practice are illustrated on page 27 of the Work Book.

Capitals and swash capitals *Work Book, pages 28 and 29*

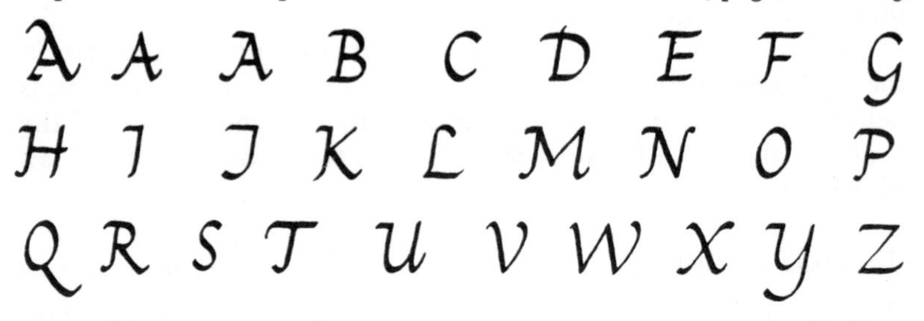

Give practice in writing capital letters with a square-edged pen. Capitals may slope forward slightly if desired, but the slope must be uniform.

To simplify instruction for young pupils, capitals have been illustrated throughout the Work Books as equal in height to the tall ascenders. They should never be larger than the tall ascenders and ideally should be slightly smaller. The more able pupils may be allowed to modify the size of capital letters in this way.

After all capital letters have been written a few times, further practice should be concentrated on the letters which are written least well.

An effective method of learning to write capitals with ease and speed is to write passages using only capital letters.

Capitals may be flourished slightly in the way illustrated on page 29 of the Work Book. Such decoration should be restrained and will be most satisfactory when pupils are writing with such ease and freedom that the embellishment of the letter grows naturally as the result of their mode of writing.

The children should now be given frequent practice in writing passages such as those illustrated on page 29. The procedure detailed for page 15 of the Work Book should be followed. Pupils should frequently assess the quality and speed of their writing.

Laying out a page *Work Book, page 30*

Discuss with the class the features of neat, attractive and beautiful writing (see Work Book 3, page 28), and let them answer the questions on page 30 of the Work Book.

By means of diagrams on the blackboard, amplify the notes given in the Work Book regarding the size of margins. Stress the advantages and the necessity of leaving reasonable margins in letters and written work of all kinds. Discuss the placing of the address on letters and envelopes, and the layout of material on all the pages of the Work Book.

The pupils should have practice in setting out material on a page and any faults in layout pointed out to them.

Writing a letter *Work Book, page 31*

Practise writing and setting out a letter and addressing an envelope correctly. The address and date on a letter may either be placed in the middle of the top of a page as illustrated or at the top right-hand corner.

Formal letters, invitations, notices, or work for display, will commonly be written in a formal hand such as illustrated, but ample practice should be given in writing a free, speedy hand with the square-edged pen.

Writing a verse *Work Book, page 32*

This page illustrates a passage in the formal, set hand. Children should have a great deal of practice in writing such passages in both the formal and free hands. They should constantly apply checks on the quality and speed of their writing. Practice should naturally be directed to removing faults which are apparent. Mere practice in writing without adequate motivation and direction to specific ends is unlikely to lead to appreciable improvement.

Think On These Things

Whatsoever things are true,
whatsoever things are honest,
whatsoever things are just,
whatsoever things are pure
whatsoever things are lovely,
whatsoever things are of
good report,
if there be any virtue
and if there be any praise
think on these things.

Specimen page from Work Book Four